Praise for *PropTech 101*

"In *PropTech 101*, the founders of MetaProp, a VC fund at the heart of the real estate industry, provide you with a 'mental map' of a rapidly evolving world. They explain how technology is fundamentally changing the entire real estate landscape, provide insightful analogies from the past, cutting edge commentary about the present, and give a systematic exposition of the likely future.

They explain how startups can engage with the industry and vice versa, and how investment strategies need updating. Wherever you sit within the industry you will be better prepared for the future after reading this book."

Antony Slumbers

International PropTech speaker, consultant, and strategist

"There is no other book that will help you gain a better understanding of where PropTech has been where it is now and where it must go. This book will help you build on the narrative that is PropTech from one of the original founders of it all. If you are involved in real estate in any way this is a must read. Don't miss it!"

Duke Long

Principal, Duke Long Agency

"New York City is the undisputed real estate capital of the world; throughout our five boroughs, we have billions of square feet in residential, commercial, and industrial properties. Our unparalleled building stick and thriving tech sector position us to be an epicenter of industry innovation, and *PropTech 101* shares insights from those leading this revolution."

James Patchett

President, NYC Economic Development Corporation

"The book puts together a comprehensive view of the thrilling, complex, growing world of PropTech using fascinating historical references, the writers' unique experience in the industry and interviews the disruptors themselves. Reading this book helps the reader draw a mental map of who and what is changing the real estate world."

Julia Arlt

Global digital real estate leader, PwC

PROPTECH 101

TURNING CHAOS INTO CASH THROUGH REAL ESTATE INNOVATION

PROPTECH 101

AARON BLOCK   ZACH AARONS

Published by Advantage, Charleston, South Carolina.
Member of Advantage Media Group.

ADVANTAGE is a registered trademark, and the Advantage colophon is a trademark of Advantage Media Group, Inc.

Printed in the United States of America.

10 9 8 7 6 5 4 3 2

ISBN: 978-1-64225-060-2
LCCN: 2019931050

Cover design by Melanie Cloth.
Layout design by Megan Elger.

This publication is designed to provide accurate and authoritative information in regard to the subject matter covered. It is sold with the understanding that the publisher is not engaged in rendering legal, accounting, or other professional services. If legal advice or other expert assistance is required, the services of a competent professional person should be sought.

Advantage Media Group is proud to be a part of the Tree Neutral® program. Tree Neutral offsets the number of trees consumed in the production and printing of this book by taking proactive steps such as planting trees in direct proportion to the number of trees used to print books. To learn more about Tree Neutral, please visit **www.treeneutral.com**.

Advantage Media Group is a publisher of business, self-improvement, and professional development books and online learning. We help entrepreneurs, business leaders, and professionals share their Stories, Passion, and Knowledge to help others Learn & Grow. Do you have a manuscript or book idea that you would like us to consider for publishing? Please visit **advantagefamily.com** or call **1.866.775.1696**.

To Dave and Phil for their tireless entrepreneurial inspiration,
mentorship, and love.

TABLE OF CONTENTS

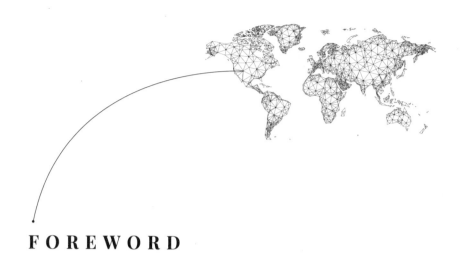

FOREWORD

Julie Samuels,
Executive director, Tech:NYC

It seems obvious now that New York City would be the center of gravity for the exploding PropTech industry, but just a few years ago that wasn't so clear. Then Aaron, Zach, and their collaborators came on the scene and saw what others before them had missed—that all the pieces were right here, waiting to be pulled together. Lucky for us, they not only saw the right strategy, but were also able to execute it.

New York has dominated the real estate world for as long as any of us can remember. We have the second largest global commercial real estate market ($657 billion, to be exact), the largest market in the United States for international travelers staying in hotels, and the metro area is the nation's largest apartment market with 2.2 million rental units.[1]

---

1   "Tokyo, New York and Los Angeles are World's Largest Real Estate Investment Markets, CBRE Research Finds," CBRE, October 19, 2017, https://www.cbre.us/about/media-center/global-stock-of-investable-real-estate; "NYC & Company Annual Summary 2016-2017," NYC & Company, accessed December 2018, https://www.nycgo.com/assets/files/2016annualsummary.pdf; "Multifamily Metro Outlook: New York Spring 2018," Fannie Mae, accessed December 2018, https://www.fanniemae.com/content/fact_sheet/multifamily-metro-outlook-quarterly-new-york.pdf.

New York is also home to a robust and diverse technology sector that employs well over 120,000 people and rivals any other international tech hub.[2] I firmly believe New York's dominance in technology will only continue to grow, as more companies are born in existing and regulated industries—industries like real estate. The days of starting a company in a suburban garage without the watchful eyes of regulators and competitors are over. Instead, the next generation of big technology companies will require knowing how to work with potential customers, clients, and competitors, not to mention governments and other stakeholders. Living and working in a city like New York provides exactly those opportunities, especially for the growing PropTech space.

The MetaProp founders saw these trends and became the connective tissue that the real estate industry needed to find its way into the modern technology economy. It has been amazing to watch what they've built and see how they've brought together countless stakeholders, from city and state agencies to major corporations and universities. Now, they are known as the go-to minds for early-stage PropTech and have solidified NYC as the global headquarters for the real estate technology sector.

What the MetaProp team has built is incredibly meaningful for the larger NYC technology sector. Aaron, Zach, and their team have capitalized on their backgrounds across real estate and tech to tell what is a uniquely New York story—the inevitable collisions of people, companies, expertise, and experiences to create the future of the technology economy.

Technology is just a tool. Knowing how to implement it at the right time and in the right place is the real trick. For PropTech, that

---

2   Greg David and Cara Eisenpress, "Tech Takes Over," Cain's New York Business, February 25, 2018, https://www.crainsnewyork.com/article/20180226/FEATURES/180229939/new-york-is-the-tech-sector-s-official-second-city-and-the-boom-is-just-beginning.

time is now, and there is no one better situated than the MetaProp team to help understand the quickly moving trends and opportunities that will shape the future of real estate here in New York City and across the globe.

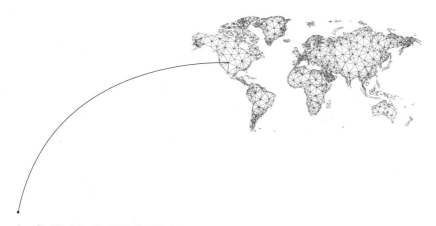

ACKNOWLEDGMENTS

As always in such an endeavor, there are many people to thank for their support and contributions to this book. We cannot mention them all here, but safe to say that anyone who is mentioned in *PropTech 101* has our deepest thanks not only for the time and effort they contributed to its publication, but also for their support of MetaProp and the global PropTech community as well. Some friends deserving recognition include Ryan Baxter, Josh Panknin, Andrew Ackerman, Ron Kravit, Josh Mendelsohn, Lance Neuhauser, Jordan Nof, Maria Seredina, Dan Hughes, Rob Keve, Joe Speiser, Tara Stacom, Mario Palumbo, Julia Arlt, Eric Thomas, Ron Gross, Shayna "Greatness" Lyandvert, Tal Kerret, Sean Muellers, Ryan Perfit, Jen Wojan, Arnaud Simeray, Al Goldstein, Taylor Wescoatt, Greg Grossman, Sarah Malcolm, Michael Warszawski, Taylor Greene, Julie Samuels, Tyler Eufer, Clelia Peters, Fred Peters, and Chris Marlin.

We would especially like to thank our long-time business partner and friend Philip Russo as well as our writing partner Barry Pierce for their extensive efforts helping to produce this book. Phil interviewed many of the people found within and also project-managed and helped edit the final product. Additionally, we owe a big thanks to MetaProp partner Zak Schwarzman as well as Iurij Cussianovich,

Tom Cashel, Evan Petitt, and the other amazing MetaProp employees who regularly contributed to this book's success.

We also owe thanks to our spouses, partners, and children who continue to support us through our late nights, weekends, and vacation-crushing entrepreneurial endeavors.

Finally, we wish to thank our entrepreneur, intrepreneur, innovator, CEO, and founder friends. We originally built MetaProp's business and communities to serve you. We appreciate all of your friendship, patience, support, and encouragement while we've pursued our PropTech "connective tissue" dreams. Today's industry would not exist without you!

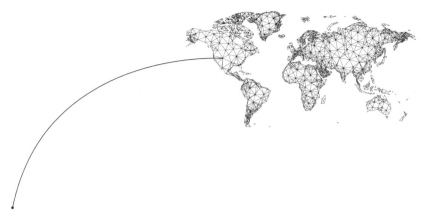

Location, Location, Innovation

PropTech, or "property technology," is rapidly transforming real estate. After decades of lagging behind on technology, the industry faces a wave of tech-enabled innovation that is reshaping the ways in which property is bought, sold, leased, financed, designed, built, managed, and marketed. Other industries, such as travel and financial services, embraced innovations enabled by mobile technology and the internet much earlier than the property sector, but because of its late start, real estate is now one of the most exciting spaces for entrepreneurs, investors, and industry leaders.

As we will explore in the coming pages, billions of dollars in capital are flowing into real estate technology. A new ecosystem of "accelerators" that help start-ups develop, partnerships that pilot new products, and events that bring stakeholders together is flourishing. Industry press outlets that treated tech as a footnote are now focusing on it, and new outlets devoted solely to PropTech have sprung up. A growing number of universities are offering PropTech courses, and researchers have begun exploring the space from a variety of angles.

The PropTech transformation is really about innovation. Technology is simply the means to an end, a way to develop new processes, systems, and tools, but its influence is being felt in every corner of the real estate industry. Real estate practitioners of all stripes, from the residential sales agent to the general contractor to the REIT executive, are facing unparalleled threats and opportunities, as the way in which they do business changes at an ever-faster pace. Those who embrace PropTech will have the chance to realize efficiencies, save money, and add revenue streams. They will have the means to get better information and perform more astute analysis, while improving customer service.

Some of those who do not embrace real estate technology will be dragged along, forced to up their game by vendors and clients, perhaps well behind the competition. Others won't survive. In chapter 8, Trulia founder Pete Flint predicts that as a result of tech advances, "most" traditional real estate agents will be gone in a decade. Robert Entin, the executive vice president and CIO of Vornado Realty Trust, told us in an interview that he thinks office buildings will be largely self-managing in five years. The technology to 3-D-print structures already exists.

We do not have a crystal ball. We will refrain here from betting on winners or making forecasts (we'll leave that to chapter 8, "The Future of Real Estate"), but there is no doubt that PropTech advances will eliminate some jobs and revenue streams and create others. Faced with the current wave of innovation, real estate practitioners can manage change or be manhandled by it, but they cannot ignore it. As Lisa Picard, president and CEO of EQ Office, notes in chapter 6, "Today, every company has to be a technology company."

Given the dizzying pace and expanding scope of PropTech, though, how can anyone hope to keep up?

Well, you're holding the first step in your hands. We hope that this book will be interesting and useful for those deep in real estate technology since it combines our expertise with that of the foremost authorities in industry, technology, and venture capital. However, it is first and foremost designed to be an introduction to the space, a primer for the uninitiated. Our intended audience includes entrepreneurs (and "wantrepreneurs"), industry leaders, investors, and tech enthusiasts, as well as media, critics, and other PropTech influencers. This is not an exhaustive look at PropTech, if such a thing is even possible, given the pace of change. It is, rather, a broad overview of basic history, dynamics, key stakeholders, and trends. Furthermore, given our base in New York City, much of our perspective is skewed to North American PropTech. However, make no mistake, PropTech is already a global phenomenon.

We have interviewed dozens of thought leaders from the US and abroad to assemble a diverse array of voices and perspectives on tech-enabled innovation.[3] They offer tips for entrepreneurs attempting to build businesses and make inroads with legacy companies as they scale. There is advice for enterprise companies piloting early-stage technology and partnering with tech start-ups, which often have workable solutions but a culture starkly different from that of incumbents. Top venture capitalists share their strategies for investing in PropTech and their criteria for assessing start-ups. We give a special

---

3   Unless otherwise noted, all quotes used are from interviews conducted by the author(s) with the respective individuals.

focus periodically on early-stage PropTech, the most rewarding and difficult part of the space, since that is our bailiwick at MetaProp.

Along the way, we'll explain what we do as an organization, not to be self-serving but because we have worked hard to make MetaProp the global nexus for real estate and technology. MetaProp's core endeavors—including investments, advice, and acceleration—reflect the key elements of the PropTech ecosystem. So, telling our story is one of the best ways we know to tell the story of PropTech.

MetaProp's venture capital funds and its principles have invested in more than ninety PropTech companies, which, collectively, have raised more than $2 billion and employ more than 1,500 people around the world. The MetaProp Accelerator at Columbia University has helped some of the most innovative early-stage start-ups grow into viable businesses, matching them with mentors and partners from the top enterprise firms. And MetaProp's advisory and consulting efforts help major players in real estate with their innovation strategies and growth goals.

Community is at the heart of everything we do, from mentoring to conducting research to facilitating partnerships to sponsoring dozens of PropTech events. As two of MetaProp's founding partners, we have a unique set of skills and experiences that makes the complex work of building bridges in this space second nature.

Aaron Block has been co-founder and managing director of leading PropTech venture capital firm MetaProp since its inception in 2015. Previously, Aaron was an executive running the Chicago region of global commercial real estate services firm Cushman & Wakefield before serving as the chairman of Chicago-based BayRu, the US-Russian e-commerce company and eBay's exclusive drop-shipping partner for Russia/CIS consumers. Aaron has served on a number of leadership boards and committees including the Young

Presidents Organization, ULI New York, NYC Community Board Five, Friends of the Chicago River, and United Way Russia.

Zach Aarons was one of the top angel investors in PropTech before co-founding MetaProp, where his team has funded more than sixty start-ups. Previously, he worked as a commercial real estate developer with Millennium Partners; an investor at ENIAC Ventures; and the founder of Travelgoat, a walking tour company. He is a professor of PropTech at Columbia University and serves on the board of trustees for the Tenement Museum. Zach is also the 2017 recipient of the NYC Real Estate Tech Week's "Investor of the Year" award and has been featured in dozens of international media publications and conferences.

Both of us have backgrounds in real estate and technology, and their intersection. We have both been investors, and perhaps most important, we have both been entrepreneurs. We know what it means to start, grow, and exit companies. This experience is critical for understanding the world of early-stage PropTech, which, as we said, is the most innovative and difficult part of the space, with the greatest risk and the greatest potential reward.

In this book, we will walk you through the thrilling, complex, rapidly growing world of PropTech. Our goal is not to show newcomers every nook and cranny of real estate technology. No book can do that. Think of this, rather, as a set of keys that we hope will open the door and let you into the space so that you can begin to explore it with confidence and a mental map of the most important contours.

CHAPTER ONE

PropTech Is Remaking Real Estate

With Sears, we're mourning a company that's been around for 126 years. It was essentially destroyed by private equity people, and the truth of the matter is, that's a company that was so far ahead of its game, like the Amazon of 100 years ago, allowing products to get into everyone's home through catalogs, right down to ordering a house. They just didn't change with the times.

—Joanne Wilson, CEO, Gotham Gal Ventures

The wave of tech-enabled innovation transforming real estate today eclipses the revolution wrought by the first skyscrapers. As in other industries, new technology and new models present both opportunities and serious threats. The latter stem from automation, disintermediation, and functional obsolescence.

The New York Home Insurance Company aimed high when it decided to build a new Chicago headquarters in the 1880s. Fireproofing was an obvious priority after the Great Chicago Fire of 1871, but so was density. The business wanted to maximize the number of offices that would be located on floors above the ground-floor bank anchoring its new building. Architect William Le Baron Jenney won the open-design contest with radical plans for a structure that would rise ten stories (later expanded to twelve), a dizzying height for the time.

How did he do it? Before the Home Insurance Building was built, load-bearing walls supported large structures. The taller the building, the thicker the walls had to be, so anything higher than a few stories became weighty, unwieldy, and dungeon-like. Jenney upended the established approach by using a frame of iron and steel to support the structure, allowing the walls to hang on the beams like curtains.

The Home Insurance Building, widely considered the first sky-scraper, owes much to Jenney's ingenuity, but it was the confluence of several cutting-edge technologies that made his revolutionary design possible in 1885. A new process for manufacturing inexpensive steel allowed him to design a building as sturdy as its neighbors but more fire resistant and with only one-third of the weight of purely masonry construction.[4] Equally important was Elisha Otis's invention of a safe, commercially viable elevator, which made working ten stories up feasible.[5] Electricity and incandescent lighting, both cutting-edge technologies at the time, were also critical.

---

4   Colin Marshall, "The World's First Skyscraper: A History of Cities in 50 Buildings, Day 9," *The Guardian,* April 2, 2014, https://www.theguardian.com/cities/2015/apr/02/worlds-first-skyscraper-chicago-home-insurance-building-history.

5   Olivia B. Waxman, "This Is the Patent for the Device That Made Elevators a Lot less Dangerous," *Time* magazine, March 23, 2017, http://time.com/4700084/elevator-patent-history-otis-safety/.

Not everyone was thrilled with Jenney's breakthrough. Some critics complained that, if replicated, such density would destroy the central business district, and others mocked the idea that anyone would want to work ten or fifteen stories in the sky. The city shut down construction on the Home Insurance Building for a time to assess whether it could really be constructed safely.[6] As more high-rises rose, the real estate industry lobbied for height restrictions in an attempt to protect the value and occupancy rates of existing office space.[7]

Over the next decade, however, Jenney's innovation proved unstoppable. By 1893, Chicago had a dozen skyscrapers of sixteen to twenty stories clustered downtown, and other cities were following suit.[8] The ability to build exponentially more useable space per block in a central location sent land values soaring in the business district, and the brokers who could assemble and control such sites profited handsomely.

Others on the leading edge of the trend profited in all sorts of ways. Richard T. Crane catered to the construction changes with new manufacturing processes, turning a one-man brass and bell foundry into a global company that produced everything from steam-boiler alarms to sophisticated elevators.[9] George Fuller made his fortune by creating a firm that could coordinate the many building specialties and the hundreds of workers needed to construct the new skyscrapers that so fascinated him.[10] We take general contractors for granted

---

6   Colin Marshall, "The World's First Skyscraper: A History of Cities in 50 Buildings, Day 9," *The Guardian,* April 2, 2014, https://www.theguardian.com/cities/2015/apr/02/worlds-first-skyscraper-chicago-home-insurance-building-history.

7   Daniel Bluestone, *Constructing Chicago,* (New Haven, Connecticut: Yale University Press, 1993): 150.

8   Carol Willis, *Form Follows Finance: Skyscrapers and Skylines in New York and Chicago* (Princeton Architectural Press, 1995), 50.

9   *International Directory of Company Histories vol. 30,* (Los Angeles, California: St. James Press, 2000).

10   *Encyclopedia of Chicago,* s.v. "Fuller (George A.) Co.," accessed August 15, 2018, http://www.encyclopedia.chicagohistory.org/pages/2678.html.

today, but Fuller pioneered the concept, outmaneuvering longtime builders who were tied to an archaic system.

The ripple effect of the inchoate skyline are hard to overstate. The steel-frame construction used in the new skyscrapers' construction, for example, allowed for larger windows, and the buildings' growing density boosted demand for consumer goods and services downtown, factors that contributed to the development of a new concept: the department store. Small merchants organized protests against the gargantuan new retailers that seemed to dominate the market overnight, but no luck.[11] Shoppers did not hesitate to jump ship for the new stores that pampered them and which provided not just shopping but *an experience* as well as unbeatable service and variety.

Increasingly, the shoppers and employees at those department stores came from small towns and rural areas. In 1850, around 15 percent of US residents lived in cities. By 1900, that number had grown to almost 40 percent, and while cities boomed, many small communities felt the economic pain of lost jobs and shrinking populations.[12]

The PropTech Wave Is Growing

This is not a history book. So why are we starting with the revolution that stemmed from the elevator and steel-frame construction in the 1880s? We might have chosen any of a number of pivotal moments in US real estate, but we believe that not since the birth

---

11   *Encyclopedia of Chicago*, s.v. "Department Stores," accessed August 15, 2018, http://www.encyclopedia.chicagohistory.org/pages/373.html.

12   Jonathan Rees, "Industrialization and Urbanization in the United States, 1880–1929," *Oxford Research Encyclopedias, American History,* accessed August 15, 2018, http://oxfordre.com/americanhistory/view/10.1093/acrefore/9780199329175.001.0001/acrefore-9780199329175-e-327.

of the skyscraper and the wave of mechanization and urbanization that followed has the industry experienced change as deep and far-reaching as the transformation underway.

As was that earlier seismic shift, the current one is driven by technology, primarily the internet and mobile technology. It is affecting every corner of the real estate industry "from dirt to disposition," to quote our friend Neil Shah, managing director of the Americas for the Royal Institution of Chartered Surveyors, from a conversation he had with us. The long list of advances that accompanied the first skyscrapers is astonishing. They involved architecture, steam heating, elevator design, lighting, plumbing, construction, urban planning, real estate sales, and financing, among other areas. Consider that the US Patent Office issued 987 patents in 1850, yet in 1890, five years after William Le Baron Jenney's breakthrough, it issued 28,299.[13] We are not suggesting that the first skyscrapers influenced all of those inventions, only that Jenney's creation was a key part of a wave of unprecedented innovation.

In 2018, as we write this, the pace of innovation is even faster because the population is much larger; markets are not just larger, but global, and speed is a hallmark of the digital age. The changes underway are structural, altering and integrating systems in fundamental and unprecedented ways in all industries, not just real estate. Don't take our word for it. Here is what Klaus Schwab, founder and executive chairman of the World Economic Forum, wrote about the transformation often called the fourth industrial revolution:[14]

---

13 "U.S. Patent Activity Calendar Years 1790 to the Present," US Patent and Trademark Office, accessed August 15, 2018, https://www.uspto.gov/web/offices/ac/ido/oeip/taf/h_counts.htm.

14 Klaus Schwab, "The Fourth Industrial Revolution: What It Means, How to Respond," World Economic Forum, January 14, 2016, https://www.weforum.org/agenda/2016/01/the-fourth-industrial-revolution-what-it-means-and-how-to-respond/.

The speed of current breakthroughs has no historical precedent. When compared with previous industrial revolutions, the Fourth is evolving at an exponential rather than a linear pace. Moreover, it is disrupting almost every industry in every country ... The possibilities of billions of people connected by mobile devices, with unprecedented processing power, storage capacity, and access to knowledge, are unlimited. And these possibilities will be multiplied by emerging technology breakthroughs in fields such as artificial intelligence, robotics, the Internet of Things, autonomous vehicles, 3-D printing, nanotechnology, biotechnology, materials science, energy storage, and quantum computing.

The ways in which real estate gets bought, sold, leased, financed, appraised, designed, managed, and so on have already changed dramatically in recent years. You know this even if you are not a real estate practitioner, since we are all, on some level, real estate consumers. Not long ago, if you wanted to rent an apartment, in most places you started with newspaper ads, a management company, or a broker. Today, in New York City alone, you might begin with a half dozen applications meant to help you find a place to live without having any human interaction, and another half dozen tech-enabled brokerages looking to minimize the human touch but which still highlight it when applicable. Each of these has unique features from interactive mapping to real-time listing to

The ways in which real estate gets bought, sold, leased, financed, appraised, designed, managed, and so on have already changed dramatically in recent years.

custom search filters that have changed the nature of the hunt and the ways in which brokers and landlords operate.

Not so long ago, when you wanted to buy a book or a blender, you went to a nearby store. Now, you are as likely to go to Amazon or another online retailer in a search that still involves real estate, only it's a warehouse on the edge of town, not a shop down the block. A real estate agent's analysis of properties comparable to yours used to be the first research most of us sought when selling a home. Now, we start with a "Zestimate," Zillow's automated online valuation, or an estimate from Eppraisal, HomeGain, Redfin, or another website.

How many of us simply call a hotel chain when traveling anymore? We book a room or an apartment with Airbnb, or use one of many online travel agents such as Expedia, Priceline, Kayak, or Orbitz. If we want to turn our thermostat down, dim lights, or listen to music at home, it's increasingly likely that Alexa or some other smart-home assistant will do it for us.

Many of the real estate innovations mentioned above already seem to be old-hat; they have become such a part of our daily lives. First of all, none of them are all that old. For instance, Zillow, which now feels like the great granddaddy of residential real estate technology start-ups, was launched in 2006 and went public in 2011. Second, despite their newness, many of them are, in a way, old-hat. The pace of transformation in PropTech has become so lightning quick that a few years can feel like a lifetime. We should acknowledge, however, that an earlier wave of real estate technology, ranging from enterprise resource planning platforms—such as those created by Argus and JD Edwards in the '70s—to CoStar's emergence online during the last tech boom, set the stage for PropTech.

PropTech is a term we should define before continuing. Note that there are many evolving definitions. For simplicity, we'll use this one:

> ***PropTech*** (also called real estate tech, RETech, or RealTech) is short for "property technology." The term refers to the software, tools, platforms, apps, websites, and other digital solutions enlisted by real estate practitioners, from brokers and appraisers to architects and construction managers. It encompasses ConTech (construction technology) and CREtech (commercial real estate technology), and overlaps with FinTech (financial technology). PropTech realizes efficiencies and facilitates real estate activities, including buying, selling, leasing, managing, appraising, financing, marketing, developing, designing, building, and investing, among others.

In mid-2016, real estate technology expanded from being a primarily US-based phenomenon to one that was clearly global in scope. As a reflection of that trend, we at MetaProp led the switch from the common label of RETech to PropTech, a term already sometimes heard in Europe.

The rapid global expansion of PropTech during just the last couple of years demonstrates how dramatically the real estate industry is changing, and the influx of venture capital into this space highlights the fact that, for all the innovation underway, we are still feeling only the tip of the spear. We'll explore investing in more depth in chapter 7, but for now, consider that in 2015 global venture capital investments in PropTech companies totaled around $1.8 billion, and in

2016 it more than doubled to $4.2 billion, and in 2017 it again *tripled to $12.6 billion.*[15]

A wave of established venture-capital funds has moved into PropTech investing, and new funds devoted exclusively to PropTech are emerging. "Accelerators," which provide mentoring, connections, and resources for start-ups, continue to grow, and the number of events, blogs, publications, and associations devoted to or including PropTech has exploded.

Every week brings news of major new mergers, acquisitions, and strategic partnerships in PropTech. It's difficult to track the high volume of start-ups working on dazzling solutions, involving everything from energy efficiency to subletting to pop-up retail space. At MetaProp, we look at one hundred to one hundred and fifty start-ups every month, and though we only invest in and mentor a small percentage of those, we're continually amazed by the creative tools, solutions, and platforms young entrepreneurs are testing.

The start-ups emerging include companies such as Bowery, which arms its appraisers with a cloud-based mobile inspection app to deliver high-quality appraisals in less time than top competitors. In New York, Triplemint has created an end-to-end property platform that allows renters to see all properties with a single agent, edging out the traditional multibroker model. A Florida-based PropTech company called Ravti is giving some building owners and managers a serious edge by lowering HVAC costs.

Many of the newest start-ups in the pipeline will fail. Many won't. If you are a stakeholder at an established real estate company, do you know which start-up might be the one that upends your business model, gives competitors an edge, or eats into your profits?

---

15 "Real Estate Tech Annual Report 2017," RE:Tech, accessed August 15, 2018, http://www.retech.net/trends/real-estate-tech-annual-report-2017.

If you are an investor, how can you determine where to place your bets in a space that's growing exponentially and changing daily? If you are a stakeholder in a start-up, or considering a tech solution to a real estate problem, how can you gauge the rapidly changing market, your competition, and increasingly complex funding options?

This book can't answer all questions for all readers, but we hope it will give you the tools to engage with PropTech in a meaningful way, to understand the basics, and to find your own answers week-by-week in an industry that is rapidly being remade.

The Techies at the Gate

PropTech has bloomed during the last few years partly because, compared to other industries, real estate was slow to adopt new technology and innovation. We will discuss this further in the next chapter, but for now, let's just say that real estate practitioners for a very long time had little reason to innovate. If it ain't broke, don't fix it, sure, but if it's broke and you're making bank anyway, you'd be a fool to fix it, wouldn't you?

In an up market—and we've had a very long stretch of low interest rates, low cap rates, and economic growth—it's easy to maintain old systems and insist on business as usual. The pace and threat of innovation, however, becomes tough to ignore when the market turns. (We appeared to be nearing the end of a cycle, for example, at the time of this writing.)

We said that real estate was slow to adopt new technology and innovation, but *was*—past tense—is the key word. Bold entrepreneurs, creative start-ups, and forward-thinking companies in all sectors are quickly making up for lost time. Real estate is the largest asset class globally, and around $38 trillion in the US alone, according to AGC Partners.[16] The openings created by an industry of this size that has lagged on technology and innovation are immense.

Thousands of entrepreneurs are providing solutions for apartment leasing, appraising, vacation rentals, construction, building management, etc. No one knows which platforms, apps, and innovations will rise to the top, but we can say with absolute certainty that the real estate industry will look very different five years from now.

How different will it look, and how will the PropTech transformation affect your business model? It might be helpful to look at a few examples from industries where tech advances already have taken hold.

- In New York City, coveted taxi medallions, once considered a virtual license to print money, were selling for upward of $1.3 million in 2013. In April 2017, one sold for $241,000, less than one-fifth of the going rate four years earlier.[17] The transformation that Uber and Lyft started will continue with green technologies and autonomous vehicles. Can cab companies, already hard-hit, survive the next wave of technological innovation? How might the big automakers have to shift in order to stay relevant and profitable?

- Every neighborhood used to have its corner video store, if not several, but Blockbuster dominated the market. Its CEO, John Antioco, saw no reason to waste good money by tying his fortunes to a start-up when the founder of a niche company called Netflix offered to sell it to him for

16   AGC Partners, "Big Data: Disrupting Traditional Commercial Real Estate Management," accessed January 2019, http://agcpartners.com/insights/manufacturing-analytics/.
17   Danielle Furfaro, "Taxi Medallions Reach Lowest Value of 21st Century," *New York Post*, April 5, 2017, https://nypost.com/2017/04/05/taxi-medallions-reach-lowest-value-of-21st-century/.

$50 million.[18] You know how this one ends. As we write this, the last Blockbuster stores in Alaska are closing, leaving exactly one in the US, in Bend, Oregon. Meanwhile, according to *Forbes*, Netflix had a market capitalization of close to $153 billion in mid-2018, greater than that of Disney or Comcast, making it the most highly-valued media and entertainment company in the world.[19]

- Speaking of media, *The Chicago Tribune* used to be one of the most respected newspapers in the country, and the Tribune Company was a highly profitable media behemoth with dozens of TV stations, interests in radio, cable TV, baseball, and more. In 2008, the Tribune Company declared bankruptcy in the largest filing in the history of American media.[20] Newsroom employment at American newspapers overall has dropped by nearly a quarter during the last ten years, according to a 2018 Pew Research Center report, and print advertising revenue has been falling precipitously.[21] On the same day in 2016 that *The New York Times* announced that print ad revenue had fallen 19 percent for the quarter, an article in *The Atlantic* reported that Facebook had announced that its digital advertising

---

18 Kate Taylor, "Blockbuster Is Closing Its Final Remaining Stores in Alaska: Here's What It was Like to Visit the Video Rental Chain before It Went Extinct," Business Insider, July 12, 2018, https://www.businessinsider.com/blockbuster-still-exists-in-a-couple-of-places-2017-4.

19 David Bloom, "Is Netflix Really Worth More Than Disney or Comcast?" *Forbes*, May 26, 2018, https://www.forbes.com/sites/dbloom/2018/05/26/netflix-disney-comcast-market-capitalization-valuation/#c44e43015618.

20 David Carr, "At Flagging Tribune, Tales of a Bankrupt Culture," *The New York Times*, October 5, 2010, https://www.nytimes.com/2010/10/06/business/media/06tribune.html.

21 Elizabeth Grieco, "Newsroom Employment Dropped Nearly a Quarter in Less Than 10 Years, with Greatest Decline at Newspapers," Fact Tank, July 30, 2018, http://www.pewresearch.org/fact-tank/2018/07/30/newsroom-employment-dropped-nearly-a-quarter-in-less-than-10-years-with-greatest-decline-at-newspapers/.

revenue had risen 59 percent.[22] Newspapers have been scrambling furiously to figure out digital advertising and online content, but for most, the effort appears too little too late.

- Hastings Entertainment, which had 123 book and media stores, announced that it was closing in 2016. Book World, the fourth largest book chain in the country, gave its notice a year later.[23] They were lucky in a sense, staving off death by e-commerce for years after the collapse of Borders. Which, of course, famously doubled down on CD and DVD sales just as music and movies were going digital. Then it farmed out its online operations to Amazon like an entrepreneurial hen outsourcing coop management to Fox Building Services, Inc. Amazon appears an ever-growing threat to all sorts of retailers (and their landlords) who haven't figured out a viable, or in some cases any, digital strategy.

We could fill this book with such examples, but you get the idea. Unless real estate practitioners want to follow in the footsteps of taxi companies and newspapers, ignoring the ways in which technology is remaking the industry is not an option. Resisting the growing wave of innovation and guarding antiquated models is as futile today as it was in William Le Baron Jenney's era, when real estate interests lobbied for height restrictions to prevent new skyscrapers from being built. Contractors who can't innovate will go the way of George Fuller's competitors, and retailers who rail against Amazon will likely

---

22   Derek Thompson, "The Print Apocalypse and How to Survive It," *The Atlantic*, November 3, 2016, https://www.theatlantic.com/business/archive/2016/11/the-print-apocalypse-and-how-to-survive-it/506429/.

23   David Streitfeld, "Bookstore Chains, Long in Decline, Are Undergoing a Final Shakeout," *The New York Times*, December 28, 2017, https://www.nytimes.com/2017/12/28/technology/bookstores-final-shakeout.html.

have as much success as the merchants who protested against the first department stores.

Instead, business owners, entrepreneurs, and professionals in all realms of real estate should learn a lesson from Borders. Keeping tabs on the tech trends likely to affect your business and building a realistic strategy that takes emerging threats and opportunities into account is more critical than ever.

Keeping tabs on the tech trends likely to affect your business and building a realistic strategy that takes emerging threats and opportunities into account is more critical than ever.

If you own or operate parking garages, for example, consider the impact autonomous vehicles will have on your business. Self-driving cars will be on the road "in a noticeable way" by 2020, according to Loup Ventures Managing Partner Gene Munster. He estimates that by 2040, 95 percent of new vehicles sold will be fully autonomous.[24] Will the whole idea of individual car ownership fade? Will the parking garage disappear or exist only to serve fleets for the Ubers and Lyfts of the world?

If you own, manage, or lease mall space, do you have a digital strategy that addresses the continuing decline in traffic? You should. A 2017 report predicted that up to 25 percent of American malls would close within five years, and that online sales would more than double to 35 percent of all retail sales by 2030.[25]

PropTech companies such as OfferPad, OpenDoor, and Knock are now buying and selling homes through sophisticated online

---

24   Gene Munster, "Here's When Having a Self-Driving Car Will Be a Normal Thing," *Fortune*, September 13, 2017, http://fortune.com/2017/09/13/gm-cruise-self-driving-driverless-autonomous-cars/.

25   Chris Isidore, "Malls Are Doomed: 25% Will be Gone in 5 Years," CNN Business, June 2, 2017, https://money.cnn.com/2017/06/02/news/economy/doomed-malls/index.html.

platforms that do work once performed by real estate agents. How might their growth affect agents and brokerages committed to maintaining a traditional sales model?

ProptTech Pressure Points

Before we explore how some PropTech companies are making waves within various asset types, let's touch on some of the broad ways that PropTech is transforming the tools, processes, and systems real estate practitioners have relied on for decades, often with little change. (We'll present a more detailed taxonomy of PropTech and dig deeper into its dynamics in chapter 4, "Defining and Exploring PropTech.")

Businesses and real estate practitioners who ignore PropTech face three broad categories of threat:

1. AUTOMATION

A 2017 study by McKinsey Global Institute predicted that automation could eliminate up to seventy-three million US jobs by 2030.[26] Economic growth and innovation will create others, but the shake-up will be painful. Advances in robotics and other technologies are eliminating jobs in everything from cleaning to security to document handling. Companies—and, in some cases, entire categories of work—are likely to disappear due to automation. Already, much of the analysis that used to be done by brokers or other staff in real estate is increasingly performed by software. Much of the data that management companies collected at buildings can now be transmitted automatically by sensors and then integrated and analyzed

---

26 Paul Davidson, "Automation Could Kill 73 Million U.S. Jobs by 2030," *USA Today*, November 28, 2017, https://www.usatoday.com/story/money/2017/11/29/automation-could-kill-73-million-u-s-jobs-2030/899878001/.

by software, all controllable from a dashboard accessible by laptop, cell phone, or tablet. Earlier, we discussed some of the many ways autonomous vehicles might affect real estate. Autonomous construction is also advancing rapidly. How will contractors who can build entirely with robots or 3-D-print whole structures affect rivals relying heavily on human labor? These and other automation efforts sometimes feel like the stuff of sci-fi. A California company called Dynasty, for instance, offers an artificial intelligence leasing agent named Lisa (Get it? PropTech certainly has a fun side) that adapts to learn your existing portfolio software and "runs your leasing business while you sleep."[27]

2. DISINTERMEDIATION

An enormous amount of profit in real estate is earned by middlemen: brokers, leasing agents, deal makers, attorneys, property managers, etc. *Disintermediation* is a fancy word for the elimination of the middleman from the process. It is a hot topic in PropTech because, some think, the right platform could eliminate the need for many if not all brokers, leasing agents, and other intermediaries, removing a layer between buyer and seller, landlord and tenant, and so on. The instant buyers, or iBuyers, we mentioned—OpenDoor, Knock, OfferPad—make instant offers for homes, based on their automated online valuations, and can purchase properties without paying a sales agent's commission. Consumers commonly get mortgages online now, without the services of a local mortgage broker, and a number of platforms can connect office tenants directly with landlords. The reality is that brokers are still involved in most types of deals,

---

27 "Company," Dynasty, accessed January 2019, https://www.dynasty.com/company.

but the roles of intermediaries are changing and, in certain niches, disappearing.

3. FUNCTIONAL OBSOLESCENCE

Real estate practitioners use this term for dated buildings that have outlived their usefulness. The structures have designs or elements that are no longer practical, utilitarian, or desirable in the current market. This label also applies to those in the industry so rooted in obsolete systems, tools, or offerings that their survival is tenuous. Could you imagine renting office space in a building that didn't have high-speed internet access? We are moving into an age in which appraisers who rely on notebooks for inspections, real estate agents who don't have a customer relations management (CRM) system, and property managers who roam basements reading meters, will appear equally anachronistic.

As we'll see in later chapters, the utility that PropTech provides is enabled by technological advancements, but these are merely a catalyst for fresh ideas and the means to an end. The PropTech transformation is really about a new mind-set, one that values a culture of innovation and is centered on the customer experience. If our start-ups are also upstarts, it's not because of dazzling digital tools but because they view real estate as more of a service than a product. They think that information should be transparent and widely available. They value speed and efficiency. They want awkward

> *The PropTech transformation is really about a new mind-set, one that values a culture of innovation and is centered on the customer experience.*

and time-consuming transactions to take place online with the same ease that they now have in other industries. They aren't afraid of the new, though many are focused on providing tools that improve existing systems and processes.

The fact that real estate managed to insulate itself from technological advancements and innovation for longer than most industries only means that the pace of change is that much faster now. Ignoring the PropTech transformation is not an option, and those who attempt to bury their heads in the sand risk irrelevance. No one is immune to the threats of automation, disintermediation, and functional obsolescence. As we'll explore later, engaging with PropTech is also a way for professionals to realize efficiencies, find new profit centers, offer more value, and gain an edge over the competition.

It's impossible for real estate practitioners to track all of the changes being created by PropTech, but an awareness of broad trends, key players, and how both are shaping a particular niche is vital. By way of an introduction, here is a quick look at how a handful of general trends and particular PropTech companies are affecting various asset types.

OFFICE

The office market is evolving quickly. The ways that information is gathered, managed, and analyzed are changing, as are the ways that space is leased and configured. In fact, the whole notion of office space—how it looks, where it's located, how it's valued, the services it offers—is shifting.

In 2016, PropTech companies VTS and Hightower merged in a closely-watched deal worth $300 million to create a leading commercial real estate leasing and asset management platform, under the name VTS. The combined companies have produced a powerful software solution that centralizes data and workflows for landlords, brokers, investors, and others in the commercial space.

In mid-2018, around eight billion square feet of office space, or nearly one-third of all US office buildings, was managed on the VTS platform. That volume gives the newly-merged company incredible leverage. CEO Nick Romito has said he wants VTS to become the Bloomberg terminal for commercial real estate, *the place where everyone goes to find key information and to communicate, from local-market players to top institutional players.*[28] To that end, the company launched a new product called VTS MarketView, which provides market trends analysis using the wealth of data that VTS already generates.

Landlords, investors, and brokers with access to the kinds of efficient tools and real-time data provided by VTS and other PropTech companies are likely to have an edge over less-tech-enabled competitors.

Landlords and managers tied to a traditional office model are also facing challenges from companies such as WeWork, which are broadly redefining the role and nature of office space in the context of the so-called sharing economy (more on this later, but think of Airbnb's apartment sharing, Uber's ride sharing, etc.). The basic premise behind WeWork is simple. Many businesses and workers today do not want to be tied to long leases and oppressive spaces with cubicles, fluorescent lights, and bad coffee. At its most basic level, WeWork merely leases space, fixes it up, provides refreshments, and sublets it.

---

28 The Registry, "VTS: Growing by Leaps and Bounds," April 27, 2017, https://news.theregistr-yps.com/vts-growing-by-leaps-and-bounds/.

The real story, and WeWork's appeal, of course, is more complicated. Founders Adam Neumann and Miguel McKelvey envisioned work spaces that would be not just communal but social and fun, flexible and creative, with leasing options centered on the customer, not the landlord. They rolled out spaces with vibrant colors, warm lighting, gourmet coffee, craft beer, and comfortable furniture (including, of course, couches). The concept expanded to include gyms, yoga classes, wine tastings, restaurants, spas, and all sorts of social interaction.

With WeWork, an individual can get limited access to a desk in a communal setting for less than $50 a month. Some large corporations, including the likes of GE and Samsung, are paying the company millions annually for large spaces, and businesses in between are choosing a wide range of price and space options. How will this reimagining of the office affect large landlords tied to vanilla spaces and long, inflexible leases? How will the industry value buildings full of month-to-month leases rather than locked-in, ten-year cash flows? The new model upends the entire value chain.

A WeWork space is not for everyone, but the appeal of the brand after just eight years is garnering serious attention—and cash. In 2018, the company was valued at $20 billion and had a network of more than two hundred co-working spaces internationally.[29] Neumann and McKelvey have moved their communal work construct into the residential sphere with WeLive and formed Rise, their health club brand. WeWork has acquired the social network Meetup and Conductor, a content-marketing platform, and it's beginning to purchase and build its own properties, not only leasing others'.

---

29 David Gelles, "The WeWork Manifesto: First, Office Space. Next, the World," *The New York Times*, February 17, 2018, https://www.nytimes.com/2018/02/17/business/the-wework-manifesto-first-office-space-next-the-world.html.

The biggest PropTech story of 2017 was SoftBank's $3 billion investment in WeWork (with another $1.4 billion going to its subsidiaries).[30] SoftBank chief Masayoshi Son is betting that WeWork's already rapid growth is just the beginning and, reportedly, told Neumann that if he thinks big, the company could be worth hundreds of billions of dollars.[31]

HOSPITALITY

Hotels have been feeling the effects of PropTech keenly during the last decade as online travel agents (OTAs) such as Expedia, Priceline, Orbitz, and Kayak have become the way so many of us now search for hotel rooms. Aggregators such as these make price and feature comparisons much easier. They make booking a snap, and through commissions, they eat into hotel profits. In terms of available space, sites ranging from HomeAway to VRBO are building on the business that Airbnb created when it rolled out a smart, easy platform that matched travelers with people who want to let apartments, homes, or spare rooms for short stays.

Airbnb has been a significant disruptor for hotels, which were taken off-guard by a start-up that grew enormously in just a few years. The Airbnb effect is especially strong at peak times and places, which once created substantial margins for hotels. The space added by Airbnb and others can exert downward pressure on prices and profits that might have skyrocketed under high-demand conditions.

30   Alex Konrad, "WeWork Confirms Massive $4.4 Billion Investment from SoftBank and Its Vision Fund," *Forbes*, August 24, 2017, https://www.forbes.com/sites/alexkonrad/2017/08/24/wework-confirms-massive-4-4-billion-investment-from-softbank-and-its-vision-fund/.
31   Steven Bertoni, "WeWork's $20 Billion Office Party: The Crazy Bet That Could Change How the World Does Business," *Forbes*, October 24, 2017, https://www.forbes.com/sites/stevenbertoni/2017/10/02/the-way-we-work/#283a40621b18.

The hotel industry has not been quite sure how to respond to Airbnb. There are efforts to lobby for tougher regulation to slow the runaway giant, and there are attempts to improve hotel offerings with more "experiential" approaches. Many boutique hotels and bed-and-breakfasts joined forces with the platform and began posting rooms on Airbnb years ago. As with many successful start-ups, Airbnb's innovation has outpaced regulatory and taxing bodies, and the dust in this space is far from settled.

The hotel industry's response to the OTAs has been even more conflicted. As Jeff Weinstein, editor of the trade publication *Hotels,* pointed out in an interview with *The Atlantic,* hotel chains gladly delivered inventory to online platforms in their early days, when vacancy rates were high.[32] Now, years later, hotels feel they need the traffic that these aggregators drive but resent the control they must cede and the rising commissions they pay for the exposure. Some hotels have fought back by encouraging direct bookings on their sites. (See Marriott's "It Pays to Book Direct" campaign and Hilton's "Stop Clicking Around" marketing effort.[33])

Based on the number of eyeballs reaching websites and apps such as HotelTonight, however, it's unlikely that large numbers of consumers will return to hotel chain websites from the aggregators. This mobile app lets users find hotel rooms up to a week in advance at discounted rates, often deeply discounted, because the booking is last-minute. HotelTonight is battling much larger aggregators such as Expedia by relying on a slick interface, substantial discounts, and an argument that it is industry-friendly.

---

32   Joe Pinsker, "How the Hotel Industry Views Its Future (and Airbnb)," *The Atlantic,* September 21, 2017, https://www.theatlantic.com/business/archive/2017/09/hotels-magazine-industry-airbnb/540525/.

33   Eran Feinstein, "OTA's vs. Direct Hotel Bookings: Which Is the Leading Trend for 2018?" *Travel Daily News,* February 23, 2018, https://www.traveldailynews.com/post/otas-vs-direct-hotel-bookings-which-is-the-leading-trend-for-2018.

"Unlike those other guys, we're your partner, not your competitor," the company promises hoteliers, offering a way to move their distressed inventory.[34]

Are apps such as HotelTonight a solution or challenge for hotels? Or, potentially, both? After consolidations that left Expedia and Priceline as the giants in the space, how much power will hotels have in the future to negotiate with these massive aggregators? Can loyalty programs, an "experiential" approach, or other efforts siphon some of the OTAs' traffic back to the hotels' own sites?

RETAIL

Visits to stores dropped from 34 billion in 2010 to 17.6 billion in 2013, a decrease of nearly 50 percent, and there were more retail store closures in the US in 2017 than during any year on record.[35] As we noted earlier, a 2017 report estimated that up to a quarter of American malls would close within five years, and that online sales would more than double, to 35 percent of all retail sales, by 2030.[36]

Online shopping is the biggest factor in what some have dubbed "the retail apocalypse," and Amazon is at the forefront of the trend. The ease and utility of shopping online, where consumers can quickly find, price, compare, and purchase items with a few clicks while sipping coffee at the kitchen table is tough to beat. Online buying does mean waiting for delivery, but Amazon and other online retailers have focused heavily on improving distribution and shortening delivery times. Flex and other Amazon programs have experimented with crowdsourcing last-mile delivery, the expensive trips

---

34 "Grow Your Business with HotelTonight," Hotel Tonight, accessed August 19, 2018, https://www.hoteltonight.com/hotel-partners.
35 Ryan Jeffery, "Store Visits Drop 48% in Three Years," TM Forum, September 2016, https://inform.tmforum.org/customer-centricity/2016/09/store-visits-drop-48-three-years/.
36 Isidore, op. cit.

from warehouse to customers' homes. With the emergence of drones and autonomous vehicles, delivery is likely to improve even further, stiffening the competition for physical stores.

Another disadvantage to online shopping is the inability to physically hold the product and see it in three dimensions. Retailers, however, have been reporting for years now that many consumers visit stores to see items and then go home to order them online, where they might get a better deal or have the ability to do more research. Large retailers such as Wal-Mart and Target, however, have promoted the reverse process by encouraging online shoppers to purchase on the internet and then pick products up at a designated nearby store. This gets the item in the consumer's hand faster and eliminates the hardest part of delivery for the retailer.

Brick-and-mortar stores have not disappeared, and in a full-circle twist, Amazon is now experimenting with physical stores. An Amazon store contains books on shelves, but it's a far cry from the old-school stores it helped put out of business. Many of the volumes are displayed cover out, spaced, and lit, more like jewelry than books. Customer reviews are often posted right below items, and much of the store is devoted to various gadgets and digital products. The setup makes shopping feel a little like walking through a website.

Smart retailers are looking for ways to navigate these uncharted hybrids of online and physical shopping, and smart landlords are looking for ways to help them. Integrating online and in-store operations for a seamless experience seems more and more important, but how, exactly, are retailers to accomplish this? What sort of website, accounting and inventory system, marketing effort, digital advertising, and social media campaign will best serve these efforts? Sensors, biometrics, analytics, and other technology now allow retailers to track who is in their store (by categories such as gender, age, etc.), where they're pausing, and the products they're likely to be interested in. Such information can guide digital in-store advertising. It can be used to text coupons to repeat customers, or to suggest other items digitally—for instance, "If you like this, you might like ..."

As in the hotel space, an "experiential" approach is often cited as a strategy to combat online competition, but its meaning is still evolving. Can landlords provide digital or interactive features to help their tenants survive? Can they better calibrate their retail mix to include businesses that, generally, don't operate online—such as nail salons, yoga studios, cinemas, and art galleries—in order to draw foot traffic to those that do? Ironically, the "experiential" nature of the department store was a large part of its edging out of older forms of retail in the 1890s, when it created the model that lasted right up to the arrival of Amazon.

How will other PropTech start-ups reimagine retail as this type of property transforms? A company called Bulletin opens physical stores and lets brands rent sections on a monthly basis to sell their products. Click a button on its website, Bulletin promises, and your goods can be in one of its stores within five days. Might some merchants now operating stores survive by adapting to this model, focusing on products and not spaces? The rise in retail vacancies is also creating opportunities for pop-up stores and one-off events.

RESIDENTIAL

It would be difficult not to use Zillow as an example in our discussion of residential assets. As we write this, Zillow Group—which owns Trulia and StreetEasy, among other brands—has a market capitalization of around $9.5 billion. As an early pioneer, the company proved the potential for profit in PropTech and paved the way for today's start-ups. Zillow, with its volume, marketing muscle, proprietary valuation software, and transactional ability, has been mentioned by some as a platform that could, one day, replace real estate agents, or at least, large numbers of them.

In reality, since a substantial portion of Zillow's profit is derived from its Premier Agent program, a lead generator that real estate sales agents buy into, the company has been careful about biting the hand currently feeding it.

So far.

Zillow's new "Instant Offers" program—which, as the name implies, makes immediate offers for homes online based on its valuation algorithms—puts the company in new if inevitable territory. Zillow can't claim to be simply a media company when it is actively buying property in transactions that don't require a sales agent. (Sellers do receive a comparative market analysis from a local sales agent, whom they can opt to list with, as part of the process.) Sellers who take advantage of this program trade speed and convenience for price. Since they are selling at below-market rates, they tend to be distressed or are facing some exigency, such as a new job or a transfer.

Instant Offers and other iBuyer programs cater to a particular niche, but how might they expand or evolve? How might those new, wider iterations affect the traditional sales model, already under pressure from discount brokerages? What might their impact be on the availability of data once exclusively accessed by agents in multiple listing services (MLS)? Will some agents work with Instant Offers or similar programs for lower fees since such programs reduce their workload and they do not need to spend time on listing, marketing, or finding a buyer?

Redfin, another Seattle-based PropTech company, began life by trying to completely automate the home-buying process, sans agent, but failed. It regrouped, hiring a slew of agents and offering varying levels of service and pricing. As Redfin went public in 2017, with an initial public offering of $138.5 million, it was rolling out Redfin Now, a program that allows it to buy homes directly from sellers, as Zillow's Instant Offers does.

OfferPad and OpenDoor offer similar competing services and are using technology to streamline the long, cumbersome process of buying and selling homes. In addition to buying and managing single-family assets in bulk, OpenDoor is using technology to upend time-honored traditions such as the open house. With its "All Day Open House" feature, prospective buyers can check out a home anytime between six o'clock in the morning and nine o'clock at night with a mobile app or an access code sent to their cell phones. Again, no agent is needed to show the buyers around, and there is no hassle with scheduling appointments or trying to make a preordained open house time.

UK-based Purple Bricks offers yet another new model for residential sales by keeping the agent, who has advanced tech tools and local expertise, but losing the office and its expensive overhead. Triplemint, to some extent, is trying to replicate this model in the US.

If this seems to be a lot to track, we should say that we have hardly scratched the surface in terms of the emerging innovations in residential real estate. The only certainties seem to be that search and transaction functions will continue to move online, and agents and brokerages that can engage with PropTech, both to gauge trends and provide more service, stand a better chance in a rapidly shifting market.

PropTech adviser Mike DelPrete recently wrote that Zillow's acquisition of a mortgage brokerage on the heels of its Instant Offers rollout signals that the company is moving closer to the real estate transaction and transitioning "from search engine to service engine."[37] He concluded his article on the strategic shift with perhaps the most salient question: "Zillow is not standing still. Its business today looks quite different than it did twelve months ago. Does yours?"[38]

INNOVATION CONVERSATION

Pete Flint, Trulia founder, NFX managing partner

MetaProp: How did you come to found Trulia?

Pete: I moved from the UK to attend grad school at Stanford, and during my second year—this was in 2004—I had to find off-campus housing. I had moved to Silicon Valley to be in the center of technology, and I was astounded. I couldn't easily get information on local real estate to rent or buy—on neighborhoods, on prices. Every other industry, it seemed, was being impacted by technology, but this enormous industry—real estate—was sort of inaccessible for consumers. It was ludicrous. That was the initial catalyst.

I spent more time learning about the industry and just became excited by the opportunity, the possibility of starting a big business and solving an important problem. There were two big problems, actually: (1) how to give consumers access to information about the single most important financial decision of their

---

37 Mike DelPrete, "Zillow's Strategic Shift," Seeking Alpha, August 7, 2018, https://seekingalpha.com/article/4196095-zillows-strategic-shift.

38 Mike DelPrete, "Zillow's Strategic Shift," Adventures in Real Estate Tech, accessed August 20, 2018, https://www.mikedp.com/articles/2018/8/6/zillows-strategic-shift.

lives, and (2) how to help real estate agents transition their marketing and business from an off-line process to a digital one, on the internet.

MetaProp: You had been at the European travel platform Lastminute.com. Can you compare the tech landscape in that industry with what you encountered in real estate?

Pete: There were enormous parallels. Both had a fragmented supply base, you know, whether that's hotels and airlines, or real estate brokers. Both had some degree of technical infrastructure, the multiple listing service in real estate and the global distribution system [GDS] in travel. And there's a thing called "faceted search." In travel, that's departure/arrival, destination, price, quality, etc. In real estate, it's neighborhood, price, beds, and baths. That meant that in terms of building a product, they were actually quite similar, but a lot of it was also understanding the industry dynamics. We helped the travel industry transform by embracing the internet as a distribution channel and then helped real estate agents in the same way, making their product available to a larger audience cost-effectively. The big difference though was that, while online, travel start-ups wanted to replace travel agents; at Trulia we wanted to empower real estate agents with technology.

MetaProp: You founded one of the most successful early PropTech start-ups, and as a managing partner at venture capital firm NFX, you now invest in start-ups. What was it like trying to find capital as a start-up then and how does it compare to today's environment?

Pete: It's radically different. I remember one of the top venture investors saying to me that he understood the problem we were trying to solve and was excited about the team, but he'd never seen anyone make money investing in online real estate. He thought that there were structural reasons why it was an unattractive area to invest in. This was said to me in 2005 by a very, very successful investor. Literally, no one had built a successful online real estate company then. There was a perception within venture communities that it was almost an uninvestible category.

MetaProp: Well, thank goodness for Trulia and Zillow. You paved the way for a lot of start-ups.

Pete: A lot of people deserve credit, but in 2018, consumers have access to enormous amounts of information. They're increasingly making the decisions themselves, and that's opening up access to many choices, allowing consumers to transact in all sorts of different ways.

MetaProp: And a growing PropTech community has multiplied those choices.

Pete: I think that's true. It has scaled up as an ecosystem, so now there's talent, there's capital, there are advisors, there are customers, and it's changed dramatically. Ten years ago, there really weren't that many people who had skills at the intersection of technology and real estate.

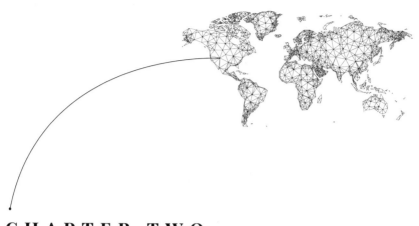

CHAPTER TWO

Why PropTech Now?

"I would have said five years ago that the industry really needs to evaluate the basic business model that has remained unchanged for decades. Now, the truth is that through competition, globalization, and new entrants to the industry, it is happening fast, and we are seeing the broad acceleration of technology, new business models, and innovative partnerships, which all create very exciting times for professionals in the industry."

—Robert Courteau, CEO, Altus Group;
parent of ARGUS Software

"I'd say that maybe being slightly early to the party was a bit of a challenge. I think we really needed to focus on early adopters, folks who saw that vision, who were interested in having these conversations, focusing on them first, and then using the success we had with those clients to get others to jump in and get them excited.

The PropTech space now—it's night and day compared to even just twenty-four, thirty-six months ago."

—Karen Maio, CEO, Nestio

Real estate lagged behind other industries in tech and innovation partly because old models remained profitable, and partly because it's hyper-local, highly regulated, and involves large privately traded assets. Catalysts rapidly helping the industry catch up include big wins (Zillow, Airbnb, etc.), new VC interest, the rise of REITs, globalization, and consumer demands.

Michael Mandel studied entrepreneurship in college and always intended to start a company. After school, he wound up working as a broker, leasing office space for Grubb & Ellis. It was reliable, commission-based work, but the job choice was a little random, since his sights were set on being an employer, not an employee. Looking around the commercial real estate industry with an entrepreneur's eye, however, he realized he'd hit the jackpot.

"What I found, working as a broker, was that if you were looking for opportunities in this industry, they were literally everywhere because it was just so antiquated," Mandel told us in an interview. "And it was, for me, a function of, 'Which one of these many opportunities that I identified do I actually want to go after?'"

The decision to focus on leasing, he told us, came during one of the painful Monday morning meetings Mandel had to sit through. He'd spent the previous night, as he spent so many Sunday evenings, frantically calling other brokers to trade "comps," details on office leases comparable to those he was working on. Exchanging that information helped brokers determine pricing, terms, and trends. It was how they stayed on top of the market. Having comps was Mandel's currency on Monday morning, even though his clients were tech and creative firms, and much of the information shared at the meeting would involve law firms, hedge funds, and private equity—leases with little relevance for him.

The system was wildly inefficient and frustrating and hadn't fundamentally changed in decades. (One of Mandel's colleagues still tracked comps exclusively on index cards, stacked across his desk in little piles.)

"My thought was, *Well, everybody's sharing this information anyway*," Mandel said of that epiphanic Monday meeting when we interviewed him. "Let's create a platform where we can share it more efficiently so that I can actually get the information I need when I need it, instead of trading random data every week."

In 2012, Mandel and his partner, Vadim Belobrovka, launched CompStak, a crowdsourcing platform for sharing lease and sales comp data. Essentially, they took the offline system for trading comps and moved it online, adding efficiencies and providing a more level playing field. Brokers, who use the system for free, earn points by anonymously adding their comps to the pool and then cash in those points (a kind of virtual currency) to peruse other comps. No more late-night calls scrambling for data; no more meetings immersed in irrelevant information.

It turns out that Mandel wasn't the only broker sick of those meetings. By mid-2018, CompStak had processed leasing comps totaling around ten billion square feet, according to Mandel, expanding to seventy markets and ten thousand cities. This does not include the hundreds of thousands of sales comps the platform also has added.

PropTech is full of entrepreneurs like Mandel who saw a gap, an unmet need, or an inefficient system in a lagging real estate industry and devised a tech-based solution to address it. Pete Flint certainly fits that bill. Looking for off-campus housing while studying for his MBA, he was frustrated by the sparse, dated real estate information he found online. That got him thinking about how the home-buying process could be streamlined, and Trulia was born. Former journalist Reza Bundy thought eBay was brilliant, but wondered why the average sale was under fifty bucks. Didn't general contractors and others want to save money on heavy equipment through this kind of platform too? They did, he learned, but given the price points, only if a qualified third party could vouch for it. He found that third party and founded IronPlanet, where inspected heavy equipment is auctioned online.

Brian Faux and Sarah Apsel Thomas, who worked together on housing issues in the Obama administration, thought that the process of getting a mortgage should be simpler and more transparent. They met with Nora Apsel and Adam Rothblatt in 2015 to talk about the prospects for an open online mortgage marketplace and wound up creating Morty. (PropTech is fun, remember?) The site offers many products from a variety of lenders without steering applicants to any particular one (a common practice in the mortgage world, online or offline), and it provides detailed information on usually opaque fees.[39]

Why Not PropTech Then?

Similar innovations happened in other industries a decade, sometimes several decades, earlier. The online travel agent Expedia debuted in

---

39 Andrea Riquier, "This Online Startup Wants to Put the 'Mortgage Guy in a Suit' Out of Business," MarketWatch, August 2, 2017, https://www.marketwatch.com/story/this-online-startup-wants-to-put-the-mortgage-guy-in-a-suit-out-of-business-2017-05-04.

1996 and went public in 1999.[40] Amazon launched in 1995 as an online book merchant, though, even then, founder Jeff Bezos knew that he wanted it to become an "everything store."[41] Online banking was built into Microsoft Money personal finance software in 1994, the same year that the Stanford Credit Union launched the first online banking website.[42] The first versions of the ATM rolled out in the '60s.

PropTech is moving rapidly today, but why has it taken real estate so long to catch up with other industries. Why PropTech now? Or maybe the question should be, why not PropTech then?

The first answer is that there was some PropTech then, or at least many years ago. Craig Newmark started a primitive version of Craigslist in 1995 and expanded with a website featuring classifieds for apartments and more in 1999.[43] CoStar, a leading data and analytics firm for commercial real estate, began as a print catalog more than thirty years ago, and then increased its utility by moving operations online. In the late '70s, JD Edwards introduced the first real-estate-focused enterprise resource planning (ERP) software to manage day-to-day business operations and analysis, and, in the mid-eighties, Argus and Yardi began providing the first purpose-built software solutions for the industry.

These and other advances paved the way for the current wave of PropTech innovations, first by showing that technology could be applied to modernize age-old systems and tools in real estate, and

---

40   "History of the Online Travel Industry Pioneer," Expedia Group, accessed August 21, 2018, https://www.expediagroup.com/about/history/.

41   Avery Hartmans, "15 Fascinating Facts You Probably Didn't Know about Amazon," *Business Insider*, August 23, 2018, https://www.businessinsider.com/jeff-bezos-amazon-history-facts-2017-4.

42   Jeffry Pilcher, "Infographic: The History of Internet Banking (1983–2012)," The Financial Brand, October 2, 2012, https://thefinancialbrand.com/25380/yodlee-history-of-internet-banking/.

43   "Craigslist Corporate History," MarketPlace, accessed August 21, 2018, https://www.marketplace.org/2008/04/21/craigslist-corporate-history.

then by showing at least some investors that money could be made in the space. Those wins were comparatively quiet, however, and didn't command attention or investment the way the latest winners have, such as Zillow, OpenDoor, and Nest.

While most people outside real estate have never heard of Argus, Zillow has become a household name. The housing platform launched in 2006 and just five years later had an IPO with a market capitalization of nearly $540 million.[44] In 2017, it reported more than $1 billion in revenue. Redfin went public in 2017, with an initial public offering of $138 million.[45] Airbnb, which began with a vague idea and a few air mattresses in 2007, made $93 million in profit on $2.6 billion in revenue in 2017, according to Bloomberg.[46]

As recent rock star start-ups have matured and begun turning profits, venture capitalists have paid close attention. Investors began to realize that the success of companies such as Uber and Amazon could be copied in real estate—a massive, largely untapped industry. Aaron certainly shared this conviction after moving from Cushman & Wakefield, where he led the commercial real estate company's Chicago region, to BayRu, which he helped grow into the eighth largest international online retailer in Russia. As a lot of entrepreneurs and investors do, he wondered why the technology, innovation, and speed that were hallmarks of BayRu had been lacking in commercial real estate.

The answer partly has to do with the risk-averse nature of the beast. Earning a living by commission produces a great deal of anxiety and a reluctance to change the business model, especially

44 Leena Rao, "Zillow Prices IPO at #20 per Share, Now Valued at Nearly $540 Million," TechCrunch, accessed August 21, 2018, https://techcrunch.com/2011/07/19/zillow-prices-ipo-at-20-per-share-now-valued-at-nearly-540-million/.

45 "Company Timeline," Redfin, accessed August 21, 2018, http://press.redfin.com/phoenix.zhtml?c=252734&p=irol-corporatetimeline.

46 Olivia Zaleski, "Inside Airbnb's Battle to Stay Private," Bloomberg, February 6, 2018, https://www.bloomberg.com/news/articles/2018-02-06/inside-airbnb-s-battle-to-stay-private.

when sales are going well. Homebuyers, who might only purchase a few properties in their lifetimes—or one—are also wary of using new methods for what's likely to be their greatest asset. How about a company leasing 100,000 square feet of office space for the first time in a decade? Whatever awkwardness might be built into the current system, for executives whose expertise lies elsewhere, this seems a touchy time to experiment.

In "PropTech 3.0: The Future of Real Estate," Andrew Baum argues that any large asset traded privately tends to resist change.[47] The fact that real estate is hyper-local and highly regulated—both factors that slow innovation—has not helped matters. Real estate also is the largest asset class, wildly diverse and highly illiquid, and historically, it's been easy to simply hold and earn, especially in an up market, which we have had for a very long time.[48] As we wondered in the last chapter, if something is broken but you're making money anyway, why fix it?

For years, the forces running real estate companies in the US weren't in a hurry to fix anything, at least not with tech solutions. Those forces tend to be old white men. Some of our best friends are old white men. We mean no disrespect, but it's perhaps not the demographic best known for rapid technological innovation. They presided over a closed system in which rigid arrangements were made on their terms, relationships ruled the day, built-in fees were protected, transactions were cumbersome, and access to information—often the key to making money—was guarded fiercely.

---

47   Andrew Baum, "PropTech 3.0: The Future of Real Estate," University of Oxford, accessed August 21, 2018, https://www.sbs.ox.ac.uk/sites/default/files/2018-07/PropTech3.0.pdf.
48   Ibid.

Tech, Culture, and the Sharing Economy

How did we go from a world in which real estate seemed archaic, to one in which it is not only rapidly catching up to other industries but, thanks to exponential increases in investment, has become one of the most exciting arenas for tech-based innovation?

Well, to begin with the obvious, without tech there would be no PropTech. The earliest advances in modern real estate technology relied on increased computing power and tools such as Excel in the '80s, and then, of course, on the internet. The overlap with FinTech was crucial, according to Baum: "The growth of indirect private fund vehicles with different styles, debt and asset-backed securitization, the arrival of REITs [real estate investment trusts], the growth of a derivatives market—all of these developments fed on and demanded a much more quantitative and research-focused approach to performance measurement and investment strategy."[49]

But those tech advances did not ripple through or alter the industry in the way that the current wave has. A more recent leap in technology, powered by cloud computing, open-source software, easier coding, the development of APIs, omnipresent mobile devices, and wide connectivity is impacting every part of the real estate value chain. In a Bisnow article that also quotes Zach on the origins of PropTech, Nathan Dever of commercial real estate tech advising company Ten-X explains the history this way: [50]

The makings of PropTech began in the mid-1980s, marked by the founding of companies that provided software for the commercial real estate industry: Autodesk

---

49   Ibid.
50   Champaign Williams, "The Beginner's Guide to CRE Tech: What Does PropTech Really Mean? 7 Industry Experts Explain," Bisnow, November 16, 2017, https://www.bisnow.com/national/news/technology/the-beginners-guide-to-cre-tech-what-exactly-is-proptech-81685?utm_source=CopyShare&utm_medium=Browse.

and NCREIF in 1982, Yardi in 1984, and CoStar in 1987. However, PropTech didn't really spring to life in a big way until the mid-2000s, when cloud computing, broadband connectivity, and mobile devices enabled residential PropTech giants RightMove, Trulia, and Zillow to launch and show investors the value of disrupting real estate through technology.

The cultural shift that occurred around this new technology and the expectations it created, fed by advancements in other industries, were as important to the PropTech transformation as the technology itself. Buying a house, for example, has long been a slow, expensive, and cumbersome transaction. Consumers accustomed to banking on their cell phones and shopping online grew increasingly frustrated by a time-consuming, largely analog process. Why do we have better tools for comparing microwaves online, they wondered, than for analyzing our next home purchase? Why do we have to go see a guy in a suit and sift through a bunch of paper to get a mortgage? Isn't there a website or an app for this? Why is this appraisal going to take so long, and why does the appraiser seem to be basing it on so little data? Why is he using a pencil?

The demands of consumers have ramped up as millennials have come of age. This is the generation that does everything online, that prefers texting to calling, and emojis to words. For them, Facebook is already passé, a site for old people. They crave the latest tech, the freshest gadget, the most powerful app. Most do not remember a time when people walked into brick-and-mortar banks to do their banking.

Members of this generation have long been renting apartments. They are also, increasingly, buying homes, leasing offices, and renting shops. They are demanding the same high level of service and convenience from real estate that they get in other spheres. A high percentage of PropTech start-ups are conceived and run by millennials, many of whom saw a slow or inefficient process firsthand and couldn't help but think of tech solutions.

Millennials are the architects of the so-called sharing economy. Many would just as soon share rides through Uber as own a car, and when they leave town, they look for shared apartment spaces on Airbnb, VRBO, or Couchsurfing. Many spend their days in coffee shops or co-working spaces rather than traditional offices. They get and assign freelance work through websites such as TaskRabbit and Upwork, and they share bikes all over the country, with services ranging from Biketown in Portland to Citi Bike in New York, and communal scooters are becoming wildly popular.

Millennials have shaped and have been shaped by the sharing economy, which in turn, has been a catalyst for PropTech. Many of the sharing companies named above are intermediaries. They match a driver with a passenger, a worker with someone who needs work done, an empty space with a laptop jockey. Typically, the company acts as middleman, usually by leveraging big data through a sophisticated, user-friendly platform.

This is a perfect model for real estate, where much of the profit, as we noted in chapter 1, revolves around intermediaries: the realtor, the commercial broker, the general contractor, the mortgage broker, and the apartment finder, among others. Once companies such as Uber proved the potential of this dormant slice of the economy, it was inevitable that others would apply the same principles to real estate. Airbnb is known by some as simply a slick middleman. That role, however, allowed it to add a massive amount of short-stay accommodations to the market: 660,000 listings in the US in 2017 and four million worldwide, more than the top five major hotel brands combined.[51] Airbnb disrupted both the hospitality and residential sectors and got plenty of attention from investors, paving the way for other intermediaries with powerful platforms able to monetize untapped assets.

Zach, who was the top angel investor in American PropTech for a reason, saw the writing early on, mapping the ways that the sharing economy and apps such as Uber's might translate into real estate. His analysis led him to invest in Breather, among many other companies. Breather is a start-up that allows anyone, from an individual worker to a large team, to book workspace through a simple app. Spaces are available in all shapes, sizes, and locations for any length of time: an hour, a month, a year. When Zach invested in Breather, the value proposition of real estate on demand—accessible instantly by phone—sounded crazy, but he was confident the trend would take hold. It did. Other players in this realm now include LiquidSpace, PivotDesk, WeWork, and Spacious, which opens up and manages unused restaurant space during the day for coworking.

Not all millennials are freelancing for Upwork in restaurants repurposed by Spacious. Some go into real estate, and this new generation of leaders, attuned to technology and eager for innovation, has helped spur the current wave of real estate technology from within the industry. They have been especially effective in family businesses, which are, typically, more nimble than giant corporations because not every strategic decision has to be debated by an enormous board.

Zach notes that a number of leaders who are about his age and who grew up in renowned real estate families on the East Coast weren't content with the status quo. They include people such as Michael Rudin, Harry LeFrak, Ryan and Joe Melohn, Mitch Moinian, and

---

51   Avery Hartmans, "Airbnb Now Has More Listings Worldwide than the Top Five Hotel Brands Combined," *Business Insider,* August 10, 2017, https://www.businessinsider.com/airbnb-total-worldwide-listings-2017-8.

Jeff and Casey Berman. Though some remain active as leaders of development, management, or other arms of the family business, they have opted to take their balance sheets and agile decision making to invest in and deploy technology. Moinian launched Currency M, a tech start-up funding division within Moinian Group. Jeff and Casey Berman founded Camber Creek, a highly respected venture capital firm that leverages their considerable real estate experience to invest in and guide PropTech start-ups at various stages of development. In addition to serving as a senior vice president at Rudin Management Company, Michael Rudin helps lead Rudin Ventures, which focuses on early-stage, PropTech start-ups.

On the home front, Zach also grew up around real estate and is part of the generation turning the technological tide. His father is a co-founder of Millennium Partners, a large-scale mixed-use developer of real estate projects in America's key gateway cities. Zach's interest in tech arose from trying to find solutions for a mobile walking-tour business he started years ago, as well as from working on social media and content marketing for Millennium Partners' development projects.

Globalization, Outside Forces

In addition to the millennials championing PropTech from within the industry, outside companies also have encouraged it, if indirectly. KPMG addresses this dynamic in its 2017 global PropTech survey, "Bridging the Gap: How the Real Estate Sector Can Engage with PropTech to Bring the Built and Digital Environments Together." As the survey reports:[52]

---

52   "Bridging the Gap: How the Real Estate Sector Can Engage with PropTech to Bring the Built and Digital Environments Together," KPMG, November 2017, https://assets.kpmg.com/content/dam/kpmg/uk/pdf/2017/11/proptech-bridging-the-gap.pdf.

Real estate lags behind many other industries—often industries that are its clients—which might become more inclined to conduct business with property firms on the same technology page when it comes to improving investment performance. This is likely to be particularly acute in retail, healthcare, and logistics, where digital revolutions are already well underway.

The survey finds that real estate decision makers are aware of tech adoption in other industries, FinTech in particular. They understand that PropTech will impact their businesses and are exploring how to catch up. Adoption, however, can be slow or patchy, or lack thorough integration. More than 90 percent of respondents in the KPMG survey said that they thought digital and technological change would impact their business, and 86 percent saw it as an opportunity.[53] This represents a significant shift in attitude toward technology in the industry, and goes a long way toward explaining why PropTech is now growing so rapidly. But in the same survey, only 34 percent of respondents said that they had an enterprise-wide digital strategy and, on a scale of one to ten, most rated their businesses at five or below for "technological innovation maturity."[54]

Other outside forces chipping away at the industry's former insularity and speeding the PropTech transformation include the environmental movement and globalization.

With the threat of global warming, building owners and management companies are under pressure to lower carbon emissions and other pollution, to conserve energy, and to reduce waste. They have turned to a branch of technology often dubbed the Internet of Things (IoT) for solutions, creating so-called smart buildings. The

---

53   Ibid.
54   Ibid.

IoT involves networks of sophisticated sensors, regulators, and other devices that can transmit data and be controlled remotely, often from dashboards accessible by cell phone or tablet.

Wiring a building for this sort of efficiency would have been difficult and prohibitively expensive five years ago. A new wave of technology makes it feasible even for small players. Realty executives who have embraced energy-related PropTech have found that it's not only the right thing to do but can significantly improve net operating income, while helping to attract and retain tenants. As Dan Probst of JLL, has argued, "smart building technology investments typically pay for themselves within one or two years by delivering energy savings and maintenance efficiencies."[55]

Realty executives who have embraced energy-related PropTech have found that it's not only the right thing to do but can significantly improve net operating income, while helping to attract and retain tenants.

As environmental concerns have become global, so has real estate. This is another trend driving the PropTech wave. As Baum writes in "PropTech 3.0": "the rapid globalization of the real estate industry in terms of investors, sources of capital, and advisory services substantially reduced the insularity of the industry and brought increased demands for a more research-led product."[56]

Just a couple of cycles ago, enormous asset managers such as CBRE, JLL, and Cushman & Wakefield had partners in Europe,

---

55   Dan Probst, "The Business Case for Smart Building Technology," Green Tech Media, October 8, 2013, https://www.greentechmedia.com/articles/read/the-business-case-for-smart-building-technology#gs.PYfBgM8.

56   Baum, op. cit.

Asia, and elsewhere, but many were not truly global firms. Now that they are, they have had to up their tech game. Some of this is synergistic. For instance, a retail trend in London now has a direct conduit to retail in Seattle or Perth. Some of it stems from client demand. The level of tech that might have satisfied the tri-state area can become inadequate quickly when you have a footprint in Singapore or Hong Kong, where expectations might be higher. A global company is only as strong as its weakest link, and so, for many major players, the stakes have risen.

The world's economies are closely linked now, and a down market anywhere, or everywhere, also tends to boost PropTech. It's easy to coast, to hold and earn, to conduct business as usual when times are good and everyone's making money. When belts tighten, everyone looks for an edge and the kind of savings and competitive advantage that PropTech offers. This effect appears to be taking hold in the US, where, after a very long stretch of very low interest rates and economic growth, rates are beginning to rise. In some quarters, supply, finally, is starting to outstrip demand, rents are plateauing, and capitalization rates are expanding. Analysts have speculated that we are at the tail end of a boom cycle.

The tech adoption that results from a softening market creates what we think of as a virtuous—others might say vicious—cycle. Real estate practitioners who see competitors adopting technology grow eager to imitate them. That spurs those first adopters to up their game, which makes the imitators up their game, and so on. Innovation begets innovation. This was true at the end of the nineteenth century, when the first skyscraper and the new technologies it relied on drove an unprecedented wave of inventions and fresh systems.

PropTech can pose a threat for those behind the curve, as we have pointed out, but for entrepreneurs and real estate practitioners who engage with it, the opportunities multiply with dizzying speed. A single big innovation—Airbnb, for instance—can birth a flurry of additional innovations and an entire cottage industry of ancillary businesses.

Building owners and management companies can ban Airbnb rentals, though their success rate will probably be similar to that of the merchants protesting the department stores emerging in the 1890s. Instead of driving short-stay rentals underground, owners can use a service such as Pillow, a tech solution that gives landlords a path to transparency, control, and a share in the revenue when residents list units on Airbnb.

Think of Airbnb as a great wooden ship of commerce. (A gold ship might be a more accurate analogy, but bear with us.) Once it hits speed, smaller, symbiotic start-ups begin to spread over the hull like lichen. The small start-ups profit from Airbnb business and, in turn, provide solutions that make Airbnb a better experience for guests and hosts. Everybody wins in a rapidly growing ecosystem that did not even exist ten years ago.

Innovation proliferation—our name for the many ways in which innovation begets more innovation—has gotten massive amounts of media attention, especially in the last two years, which, of course, has driven more entrepreneurs and enthusiasts to the space. The PropTech support systems we mentioned in chapter 1 and will explore in depth in chapter 5—accelerators, events, blogs, publications, associations, academic programs, and so on—have grown exponentially, too. They are speeding the transformation and bringing even more attention to PropTech.

The biggest catalyst, of course, has been those with deep pockets willing to invest in PropTech. A handful of venture capital firms in Silicon Valley, most notably Trinity Ventures, had enough vision early on to see the potential. Since then, as we mentioned early in this chapter, big wins of start-ups such as OpenDoor, Compass, WeWork, and Nest, as well as of older giants such as Zillow and Airbnb, have drawn capital from all over the globe into PropTech. There are many answers to the question, "Why PropTech now?" As we've seen, they are complex and interdependent, but none rates higher than the ones involving venture capital, which is why we will devote all of chapter 7 to it. Follow the money is, as usual, good advice.

Money is also the biggest source of the enthusiasm for PropTech growing within the industry. The efficiencies, cost savings, increased profits, and new revenue streams it allows real estate practitioners is unparalleled. We spent much of chapter 1, stick in hand, highlighting the threats that loom for those who don't engage with PropTech. Trading it for a carrot, we'll explore the benefits of a brave new real estate world in the next chapter.

INNOVATION CONVERSATION

Dave Eisenberg, senior vice president of digital enablement and technology, CBRE

MetaProp: What are your day-to-day responsibilities?

Dave Eisenberg: At Floored, it was traditional CEO stuff: hiring, management, executive sales support, fundraising, investor relations. At CBRE, it's a bit different because I have more of a strategic role on what we should be doing on the technology strategy side, as well as a high-level product oversight role in terms of making sure that our products are having the impact that we said that they would before we were acquired. That involves a lot of conversations with business leaders, a little bit of sales support on key pursuits. Mostly, financial planning, as well as strategic reviews of what we're doing in order to ensure that we are having the biggest impact on the company that we can. When you're an 85,000-person company, the governmental processes around unlocking dollars and people are very different than when you're running it for fifty people.

MetaProp: What is the most important innovation and technology-driven initiative in your organization today?

Dave Eisenberg: I think for us, it is the practical application of deep learning and machine learning, otherwise known as artificial intelligence, in various workflows, data collection processes, data presentation, and back-office automation. I think that we can see the best ROI on technology when it has some intelligence baked into the software. We're doing a few things to replace a lot of manual processes with thoroughly automated ones.

MetaProp: Can you assess the pace of innovation in your market and how it's evolving?

Dave Eisenberg: Certainly. I think that the pace of innovation is increasing for two main reasons. One is the people and dollars that are flowing into the industry are of a higher quality than they've been in the past, with bigger ambitions. The second is that the nature of artificial intelligence is to build upon previous iterations of itself. The more data it consumes, the better it gets. In that regard, I think a variety of AI-based software companies in the space have materially better products today than they have over the past few years, and they will again next year, which I think just clears the bar for adoption in a way that hadn't existed previously.

MetaProp: How is CBRE assessing and analyzing information differently today than it did two years ago?

Dave Eisenberg: We have a big initiative at CBRE to build out an enterprise grid, a highly secure enterprise data platform, what we call the EDP. This is the place where CBRE resolves its myriad property databases into one, such that there are single records for each of the buildings in the world that CBRE has information about. Just making that data accessible via APIs has enabled us to skip a huge amount of infrastructural work that would have been required to build effective software even just two years ago. I think without that investment and core infrastructure—and that was a two-year project, by the way—it would have been very hard for CBRE to really build cutting-edge products, which it now does.

MetaProp: You and CBRE are doing a lot of digital stuff that's really exciting. How is that innovation directly affecting the role of your professionals in your business lines and clients' expectations, as well their own?

Dave Eisenberg: I think the expectation now at CBRE is that you have a point of view about how technology is going to change the business and you have a plan of attack for how to address the change if it comes to you rather than you bringing it to the industry. I don't think that was the case a few years ago. I think that technology has permeated our lives in such a meaningful way, and especially in commercial real estate. When you think about where a lot of the growth is in the tenant types, much of that growth is in the technology sector. It's just become part of the core job. In that regard, the technology group at CBRE is a lot more important to the company than it has been in the past.

MetaProp: If you could change one thing about the real estate industry, what would that be?

Dave Eisenberg: I think this is coming, but I wish there was more of a tolerance for testing and learning on the innovation side. I think some of this is driven from the investors around using real estate as a risk-management part of their investment portfolio rather than a risk-loving part of their portfolio. I think everyone would enjoy the real estate tech ecosystem better if there was more of a culture of experimentation rather than requiring a perfect ROI story to actually get something to be adopted.

CHAPTER THREE

The Benefits of a Brave New Real Estate World

"Not raising enough cash was a factor, but it also had its positives. Being in the UK where cheque sizes are just smaller than the US market, we had to work hard for limited investment. We operated as a boot-strapped business even right up to being acquired! I do think that the 'lean' start-up model we followed was what made us a success, and I urge any other founder to be lean, boot-strapped and scrappy, even with $10 million of working capital in the bank. It makes you more resilient to ride the rough days without getting distracted."

—Edwin Bartlett, CEO and cofounder, Kykloud
(now part of Accruent, a Fortive Company)

PropTech provides massive opportunities to make money through three primary channels: information, transactions, and management/control. Start-ups ranging from House Canary to Enertiv are helping real estate practitioners build revenue with better data, more efficiency, streamlined processes, and a host of creative tools.

Let's get straight to the bottom line here, because at the end of the day, money is why you have to pay attention to PropTech. We can talk about culture change, innovation, and retention until we're out of breath. We can admonish that you should be a part of the future, that it's important to win over the millennials who will soon run the world, and that PropTech will make you cooler.

Forget about all that for a minute and consider this: PropTech can make you money.

To wit:

- **Bowery**, whose appraisers use a cloud-based mobile inspection app to deliver high-quality appraisals quickly, has, based on a recent MetaProp case study we conducted, made more than $1 million for Cushman & Wakefield since the commercial real estate firm began using the start-up's proprietary technology.

- **Ravti** estimates that its advanced software, which tracks and manages HVAC systems, can save owners of commercial and residential properties up to twelve cents per square foot annually.[57]

---

57   Ravti's website is at https://www.ravti.com/.

- **Nestio's** cloud-based platform brings all of an owner's digital marketing assets together, making it easy to distribute content to the right marketing channels on a unit level and boosting revenue by reducing customers' "days on market" by 20 percent.[58] Restaurants, which face high rents and low margins, are adding a new revenue stream with **Spacious**, a PropTech start-up that turns them into coworking locations by day, when they're normally vacant. Spacious charges workers $99 to $129 a month and shares that revenue with its restaurant partners, who also gain exposure and new patrons.

- Armed with a suite of high-tech tools, including Collections (think Pinterest for real estate) and Insights (a marketing dashboard), real estate agents reported making 25 percent more during their first year at **Compass** than they did at their previous brokerages.[59]

- **Redfin's** stock shot up 45 percent on its first day of public trading,[60] and Zillow's stock, priced at twenty dollars a share during its IPO in 2011, is north of forty-seven dollars as we write this.[61] Granted, these are the big boys, but 96 percent of respondents to MetaProp's Mid-Year 2018 Global Confidence Index said they planned to make

---

58 "Nestio Announces It Has Raised $4.5 Million in Strategic Growth Capital From Some Of The Biggest Names In Real Estate," Global News Wire, July 12, 2018, https://globenewswire.com/news-release/2018/07/12/1536655/0/en/Nestio-Announces-It-Has-Raised-4-5-Million-in-Strategic-Growth-Capital-From-Some-Of-The-Biggest-Names-In-Real-Estate.html.

59 E. B. Solomont, "Inside Compass' Recruiting Machine," The Real Deal, February 13, 2018, https://therealdeal.com/2018/02/13/inside-compass-recruiting-machine/.

60 Katie Roof, "Redfin Soars 45% after IPO; CEO Calls It 'Amazon of Real Estate,'" TechCrunch, accessed August 25, 2018, https://techcrunch.com/2017/07/28/real-estate-site-redfin-soars-45-after-ipo/.

61 Leena Rao, "Zillow Prices IPO at $20 per Share, Now Valued at Nearly $540 Million," TechCrunch, accessed August 25, 2018, https://techcrunch.com/2011/07/19/zillow-prices-ipo-at-20-per-share-now-valued-at-nearly-540-million/.

the same number of PropTech investments or more during the next year. Clearly, they are pleased with PropTech's earnings potential.

In this chapter, we will explore some of the many ways that PropTech can cut costs and make money for real estate practitioners, presenting specific examples by asset type. First, however, let's take a look at the three main activities that PropTech facilitates, according to Andrew Baum, author of "PropTech 3.0: The Future of Real Estate." There are many ways to categorize and carve up PropTech, as we'll see in the next chapter. Broadly speaking, however, Baum's tripartite division is a helpful way to think of the primary channels for boosting and creating revenue: [62]

- **Information provision.** This includes easy access to as well as integration and analysis of everything from public records to office lease data to market fluctuations to real-time boiler temperatures in the apartment complex basement.

- **Transactions.** People are used to shopping for music, buying stocks, and banking online. Increasingly, they are using the same types of fast, reliable platform, allowing for the exchange of money, goods, and services, to get mortgages, lease workspace, sign contracts, and sell houses.

- **Management and control.** Cell phones, laptops, tablets, and other devices can become sophisticated dashboards that allow for easy control of everything from high-rise heating systems to house alarms to complex portfolios. Robots performing various functions can be controlled

---

62   Andrew Baum, "PropTech 3.0: The Future of Real Estate," University of Oxford, accessed August 21, 2018, https://www.sbs.ox.ac.uk/sites/default/files/2018-07/PropTech3.0.pdf.

remotely, as can cars, drones, and other machines. Affordable, advanced sensors are as important to these efforts, which often include automation, as they are to information collection.

Sir Francis Bacon, who left his mark on science and technology, famously said that knowledge was power. He might as easily have said that it was money. Real estate practitioners used to spend enormous amounts of time and money collecting, assembling, and analyzing information. This was as true for the management company that sent workers scrambling onto roofs and into basements to read meters and gauges as it was for the asset manager paying a team to gather data on office submarkets.

Today, PropTech can deliver much of that knowledge to real estate practitioners quickly (often in real time), cheaply, and in easy-to-use formats. Advances in sensors and the IoT allow managers to track and assess building equipment and systems at a granular level from dashboards accessible by mobile devices. Companies such as CoStar, VTS, and CompStak collect and package a dazzling amount of information about commercial real estate, providing unprecedented insight into pricing and trends at all levels.

No more building engineers traipsing across roofs, and no more administrative staff gathering numbers to plug into spreadsheets.

Thanks to technology, real estate transactions have gotten easier and speedier, too, though many have a long way to go. In chapter 2, we mentioned Breather, which lets you browse and pay for workspace on your cell phone. Zach pointed out that, even five years ago, the idea of real estate on demand via phone sounded a little crazy. Not anymore. Consumers can get mortgages online in minutes. Contracts can be handled virtually, and a variety of platforms make instant payment painless.

PropTech company Corrigo, for example, has used automation to help JLL streamline invoice payment, bid management, and more, since the commercial real estate giant bought the software designer a few years ago.[63] Ibuyers, such as Zillow, OpenDoor, Knock, and OfferPad have built platforms that allow for lightning-quick sales of homes, with much of the transaction occurring online.

Transactions are an obvious place for real estate practitioners to look for tech solutions that can improve efficiency, add value for customers, and boost the bottom line.

Transactions are an obvious place for real estate practitioners to look for tech solutions that can improve efficiency, add value for customers, and boost the bottom line. Figuring out an efficient convenient way to handle a transaction is often a key part of providing a new service or unlocking a new revenue stream.

More Information, Time, Money

The speed and ease of data collection that PropTech enables obviously saves time and labor costs, boosting net operating income. However, richer, faster information, and its automatic analysis by software— tracking usage, traffic, anomalies, waste, inefficiency, and so on— allows for smarter planning and strategy, which can boost income on an even bigger scale.

Energy savings are a key benefit of PropTech, and one that can often be realized quickly. Detailed data about how a space is used, lighted, cooled, and heated, and the ability to automate or remotely

---

63   JLL, "Innovative, Entrepreneurial Company Expands JLL's Facility Management Offerings," news release, December 21, 2015, https://ir.jll.com/news-releases/press-release-details/2015/JLL-Completes-Acquisition-of-Technology-Pioneer-Corrigo/default.aspx.

control the built environment make for a powerful combination. This sort of information and analysis moves landlords and management closer to the customer, allowing them to present real estate as a service, not a product, which increasingly gives them an edge over the competition.

The growing transparency and availability of data has a democratizing effect and makes service ever more important. Much of commercial brokers' value used to lie in their relationships with other brokers and their access to information. The person with the best comps won. Residential sales agents were hired in part because they had exclusive access to a jealously guarded MLS and deep local knowledge. As technology makes such information readily available, those who can differentiate themselves with deeper analysis and smarter strategies—and prowess in deal making and marketing—stand to make more money. Paradoxically, PropTech is at once leveling the playing field and providing the means to rise above the crowd.

The resources that a commercial real estate brokerage once devoted to gathering information and plugging it into spreadsheets can now be devoted to deeper market analysis, planning, and strategy. Residential sales agents have lost the power that exclusive access to the MLS once gave them. Can they replace it with a forward-looking online advertising strategy, a suite of powerful digital tools, and a comparative marketing analysis (CMA) that harnesses data in ways their competitors' CMAs don't?

Real estate practitioners who can't adapt to innovation and who remain tied to old models will face financial challenges as paradigms continue to shift quickly after decades of stasis. Those who engage with emerging technologies and the opportunities they present to innovate, boost income, and add new revenue streams will find so many that they will be forced to prioritize them.

This is no exaggeration, just an honest assessment of the pace of innovation today from two people who are immersed in early-stage PropTech and who are astounded every week by the creative ideas that come across our desks. Some of those concepts become start-ups such as Sonder or WhyHotel, companies that monetize the empty units in new apartment buildings by opening pop-up hotels on site, with the usual guest services and the added perks of luxury apartments. The business provides a welcome revenue stream for developers who, typically, carry hundreds of empty units during the months between building completion and full lease-up. WhyHotel, for example, shares in utility costs, and new tenants like the fact that they don't have to live in a half-empty building.

Those who engage with emerging technologies and the opportunities they present to innovate, boost income, and add new revenue streams will find so many that they will be forced to prioritize them.

MetaProp backs only a small percentage of the start-ups such as WhyHotel that come to us for funding or mentoring, but many of the concepts that we take a pass on are creative and worthwhile. There are simply too many good ideas, too many opportunities for saving and making money to pursue them all. As we noted, real estate practitioners who begin paying attention to early-stage PropTech will soon face the same challenge. However, being forced to choose among innovative solutions for the ones likely to yield the best return is a terrific dilemma for any organization.

The key is to get in touch with the newest and most innovative PropTech at a level that allows you to make informed decisions. No one wants to follow the example of Blockbuster turning down an offer to buy Netflix, or of Borders outsourcing online operations to Amazon in order to focus more on DVDs and CDs. Later, we will explore some of the best avenues for getting up to speed in the rapidly changing world of real estate technology: the key events, blogs, associations, advisors, and newsletters.

Meanwhile, here is a small sampling, organized by asset type, of the innovative start-ups helping real estate practitioners realize efficiencies, lower costs, increase income, and find new sources of revenue. Our list leans heavily toward start-ups that we have worked with simply because we know them best. We only fund or mentor the concepts that we feel have the most potential, so our portfolio is a natural place to go for examples in the ever more crowded PropTech universe.

Residential

If we haven't said it ourselves, we all know someone who complains that residential real estate is full of exorbitant fees and people who don't earn their keep. Many of the trends in this asset type that are underway address that impression by improving the customer experience, using technology to enhance searches, speed up transactions, and lower fees. Technology is aiding professionals in the space, too, with systems that do everything from save energy to streamline repairs.

A company called Lemonade is turning the conventional insurance model for homeowners and renters on its head, helping to remake an industry ripe for reinvention. Why do we say this? Well, the usual insurance model is built on glaring conflicts of interest. Consider that every dollar an insurer pays a customer who files a claim is one less dollar that the insurer earns in profit. Most insurance companies make money when denying claims, which can lead to delay and distrust.

Lemonade is not powered by brokers, but by bots—an AI-based system that allows for greater transparency, ease, and speed. With its app, the company claims customers can get insurance within ninety seconds—from $5 a month for renters and from $25 a month for homeowners—and get paid for claims within three minutes.

Beneath the company's technical prowess is an innovative new model. Lemonade charges flat fees, to eliminate the usual conflict of interest. Once those fees are paid, customers' money is treated as their own and put into a pool from which claims are paid. Leftover or unclaimed money goes to a preselected cause of the policy holder's choice. This might sound like a marketing gimmick, but Lemonade is a certified B corporation, independently verified as meeting high standards for transparency, ethics, and social benefit.

House Canary is also leveraging technology to build a new model in residential real estate. The company uses machine learning, predictive analytics, and sophisticated data integration to provide advanced home valuations. House Canary's PhD statisticians and data scientists claim to have assembled the most comprehensive dataset in the marketplace to serve appraisers, lenders, real estate investment firms, and others who need to value residential property. The company's data analysis is both hyper-local, tracking specific details about a given home, and extremely broad, taking macroeconomic factors into account. Its processes have evolved to deliver impressive value reports that allow clients not only to determine current values but also to forecast three-year returns and to set rents, benefitting the bottom line with better analysis.

Radiator Labs, too, says it can benefit the bottom line through lower operating costs, saving landlords up to 40 percent in annual heating bills for owners of buildings with steam heat. Its "Cozy" is a smart, insulating enclosure installed over existing radiators. In building-wide installations, the system redistributes steam flow, transferring wasted heat from hot rooms to colder ones.

The Cozy is easy to install and requires no contact with the plumbing system or steam. The energy saving is the headline for landlords, although they're also likely to benefit from the app that allows tenants to control their own apartment temperature from an iPhone or Android. Anyone who has ever lived in an old steam-heated apartment, where temperatures tend to be extreme and impossible to regulate, understands the utility of this PropTech innovation for many hundreds of thousands of apartments.

To meet regulatory requirements, landlords usually cater to the coldest rooms in a building. Tenants closest to the boiler often feel as if they're renting in hell, while those on high floors wish they had more heat. As a result, about 30 percent of steam heat is wasted in the US, according to NYSERDA, at a loss of more than $7 billion in waste.[64] The Cozy aims to lower that waste, and, since the simple white enclosure is cool to the touch, it can also be used as a shelf.

Other innovative PropTech companies in residential real estate include Flip, a platform that helps renters get out of their leases and sublet their apartments. Flip will vet applicants, so the renter doesn't have to, and prepare rental applications and sublease agreements. For landlords, Flip offers transparency, credit checks, and automated,

---

64 "A Focused Demonstration Project: The 'Cozy' by Radiator Labs," NYSERDA, no. 18-12, May 2018, radiatorlabs.com/wp-content/uploads/2018/10/Radiator-Labs.Cozy_.NYSERDA-Report.2018.pdf.

guaranteed rent payment. As many start-ups do, Flip uses technology to become a more efficient—and in this case, safer—intermediary in a process that's often tense for both landlords and tenants. Jetty uses tech similarly to manage risk and become an intermediary, upending old models. In addition to offering renters insurance and other services, Jetty replaces the standard security deposit, which tenants often forfeit, with a smaller, one-time fee of 17.5 percent of the deposit amount.

Commercial

Commercial real estate lagged behind residential in adopting technology. However, it's beginning to catch up, driven by client demand, stiff competition, and the forces of globalization. Emerging innovations involve everything from better construction management to richer market analysis to energy efficiency.

As many PropTech start-ups do, Enertiv uses IoT technology to improve efficiency, monitoring, and control, saving building owners money in the process. The company digitizes a building's physical infrastructure to streamline all levels of operations and maintenance. Circuit-level sensors track critical equipment, such as boilers, chillers, and elevators, as well as tenant space.

The Enertiv system analyzes a wealth of automatically transmitted data, traces anomalies to equipment faults, and translates those problems into money-saving recommendations spelled out in concrete terms. For instance, HVAC managers who have to address a heat pump problem might get a message on their phone calculating that replacement would reduce runtime by six hours per day for an annual savings of $4,282.

Having worked through more than three billion hours of machine data while fine-tuning its system, Enertiv has endless case studies to show clients. In one, an analysis that revealed condenser water pumps' weather dependence resulted in the suggestion that the schedule should be changed to better align with occupancy and outside air temperatures, saving $36,000 annually. Operational improvements and retrofits at another building saved 20 percent in annual operations costs, according to Enertiv, with a payback period of four years.[65] Overall, Enertiv estimates that its OPS platform reduces operating expenses by 7 percent on average, creating around $12 of asset value per square foot.[66]

Real data management (RDM), creates value for commercial real estate companies partly by shifting unwieldy in-house operations to its platform, which streamlines leasing, building, and management processes. RDM's flagship property and space management software, RealAccess, is a high-powered repository of interactive floor plans, documents, stack diagrams, and analytics. It allows for faster and more extensive analysis, with drawing tools, overlays, and space configuration options all easily accessed online. Property owners, investors, managers, and brokers can seamlessly integrate RDM's SaaS (software as a service) solutions into their existing accounting and other systems.

Another SaaS company, Workframe, provides a workflow optimization solution purposely built for the commercial real estate industry. Large corporate tenants, landlords, brokers, and service providers gain a new level of insight into their workflows, overseeing multiple projects and locations simultaneously to measure progress on key initiatives across a portfolio. Comprehensive task manage-

65 "Case Studies," Enertiv, accessed August 29, 2018, https://www.enertiv.com/resources/case-studies.

66 Enertiv, https://www.enertiv.com/.

ment allows for transparency and prioritization, keeping teams' attention focused on the most important deliverables. Floor plans and important documents are easily uploaded and accessed to turbocharge the decision-making process. Whether it's used for portfolio management, facilities maintenance, or new construction projects, Workframe's platform drives efficiency and cost savings.

Information continues flowing just as fast, and perhaps more furiously these days, once construction projects are completed. Apart from internal data and whatever could be gleaned from other brokers, CoStar Group (which bought Loopnet in 2012) was long *the* place to go for comps, pricing trends, and other market data in commercial real estate. Newer players such as CompStak (featured in chapter 2), Reonomy, and VTS (merged with Hightower) are now providing competition in a battle that has involved several lawsuits, as well as charges of stolen information and monopolistic practices.

Knowledge clearly is money as well as power, but how are brokers and other players in the commercial space to know who provides the best data and analysis for their needs? Will a single global platform emerge? Will the space fracture even further? We don't have the answers, but the contest to provide the best commercial data highlights the direct link between engagement with PropTech and profit.

Hospitality

With its scale, often thin margins, and built-in peaks and valleys, the hospitality industry is an obvious place to find profit through PropTech. A small measure improving energy efficiency or boosting customer loyalty online can turn into serious revenue when applied across hundreds or thousands of rooms and an army of customers.

In chapter 1, we mentioned that PropTech start-ups such as HotelTonight, which reduces distressed inventory by offering last-minute discounts, can boost hotels' income. However, some luxury brands are reluctant to let their most expensive suites through discount websites. Suiteness has taken a novel approach, generating revenue for some of the top hotels in the world while protecting their brands by offering expensive suites through a members-only model. The company's hotel partners include exclusive brands such as Four Seasons, Park Hyatt, and Shangri-La, with suites available in major cities including New York, London, Las Vegas, and Los Angeles.

Guests enjoy concierge services once they arrive at their luxury hotels, but Suiteness also supplies its own personal online concierges for all bookings. As are their counterparts at hotels, these concierges are available to answer questions, arrange difficult dinner reservations, and book shows. Suiteness has exclusive deals with hotels on select suites that are not accessible anywhere else online. As professionals in the hospitality industry struggle with their digital strategies, Suiteness demonstrates that technology in this sector is about much more than simply convenient bookings and discounted rates.

Rosie offers another example of creative technology cutting costs for hotel operators. An autonomous floor cleaner, Rosie is the first offering from Maidbot, a young PropTech company that's working to automate commercial cleaning and housekeeping tasks. Rosie cleans faster than a human and collects actionable data about the building environment and operations, allowing operators to save money and improve the guest experience. Commercial cleaning positions are tough to fill and maintain, so Rosie augments the labor pool in important ways and cuts down on the highest variable cost in a hotel: housekeeping. Rosie also cuts down on injuries, which room attendants suffer at the highest rate in the service sector.

For years, we've been watching the Roomba clean with ease in homes with a couple of carpeted rooms. Considering the savings that hotels with hundreds or thousands of rooms might realize by automating housekeeping, Rosie is one of those PropTech solutions that might leave observers wondering why this idea did not *start* in hotels. The similarly named Roxy elicits comparable questions. How did Alexa get into homes, where we're comfortable, before an in-room concierge arrived in the unfamiliar hotels where visitors desperately need a voice assistant?

Roxy allows guests to make calls, order room service, arrange transport, stream music, check the weather, get a wakeup call, check out, and more, all via voice command. A single sleek device replaces alarm clock, guest booklet, speaker, charging ports, and the phone, one of the most expensive and least used pieces of equipment in a hotel room. How many people under seventy have landlines these days? Isn't it odd that nearly all hotel rooms still rely on them? Roxy promises to improve operational efficiency, too, lightening the load of desk staff and concierges so that they can focus on more value-adding tasks.

As we mentioned in chapter 1, technology has disrupted the hospitality industry in significant ways. Is Airbnb a mortal foe, or are there ways to harness it for profit, as some boutique hotels have? With high traffic and high commissions, online travel agents such as Expedia and Kayak have been both profit centers and a serious cost. How can hotels and others strategize to keep that equation in the black? Again, we can't say we have the answers, but we're confident they will involve being savvy about early-stage PropTech.

Retail

E-commerce has elevated what consumers expect from a retail experience in all sorts of ways. Demands regarding the amount of information available about products, the ease with which customers find them, and the speed with which they can be purchased have ramped up. To cut costs and increase profits, smart retailers are enlisting technology, much of it relatively affordable, with measurable results and a high rate of return.

Hointer is a good case in point. The start-up began as a denim shop in Seattle, hoping to help men find the perfect pair of jeans. Noting how much customers hated sorting through messy piles of clothes for the right size, waiting to be helped, and standing in checkout lines, the proprietor, Nadia Shouraboura, began exploring ways to combine the convenience of online shopping with the tactile advantages of a brick-and-mortar store. (It didn't hurt that she had been on the senior leadership team at Amazon.)

She transformed the sales floor into a showroom, with just one of each item, and built a micro-warehouse in the back. Shoppers used an app to select a style and size in the fitting room, and within thirty seconds, the item was delivered via a chute. The number of fittings rose exponentially, and so did sales. Hointer opened more stores, from San Francisco to Singapore, expanded into groceries and other products, and now provides tech solutions to retailers. As with much PropTech, control is key. Hointer's platform allows shoppers in physical stores to use their cell phones as they might online, quickly searching, finding what they want, and having it delivered to them rather than having to rummage through shelves.

Hointer's personalized recommendation system delivers suggestions to consumers in key decision-making zones, such as fitting rooms and test areas. Massive amounts of product information are available digitally, as it would be online, and the interest of customers who tap a digital display for a product is recorded the way clicks are in e-commerce. Hointer also supplies a sophisticated customer relations management system and helps retailers collect and analyze shopping activity to optimize process and inventory.

Hointer's early retail experiments led to six times more items being tried on and an 80 percent increase in sales.[67] Since then, the start-up has worked with leading retailers around the world, including Macy's, where automated item selection and delivery made enough space to showcase 60 percent more styles in the same physical footprint.[68]

Spacious, which we mentioned briefly above, does not lower costs or improve efficiency but creates a much-needed stream of new revenue for restaurants. The start-up, which has plans to expand from New York and San Francisco to other cities, turns stylish dining destinations into coworking locations by day, when they're normally vacant. Customers pay between $99 and $129 a month, and Spacious cuts its restaurant partners in on the profit. Workers get unlimited gourmet coffee, powerful Wi-Fi, and a much more comfortable setting than the typical office provides.

This start-up is yet another example of PropTech's penchant for innovation, intermediation, and monetization of unused assets. More than two thousand restaurants in Manhattan and Brooklyn are closed before six o'clock every night, Spacious Cofounder Preston Pesek told us in an interview. Many of those restaurants survive on thin margins and could use extra income. Armies of workers who

---

67   Allegra Burnette, Leah Buley, Tony Costa, Andrew Hogan, and Deanna Laufer, et. al, "Digital Customer Experience Trends, 2016," Forrester, December 14, 2015, forrester.com/report/Digital+Customer+Experience+Trends+2016/-/E-RES127301#.

68   Ananda Chakravarty et. al, "The Future Of The Digital Store," Forrester, April 13, 2018, forrester.com/report/The+Future+Of+The+Digital+Store/-/E-RES119167.

either do not have offices or who frequently work outside them are hungry for space, as anyone who's been in a jam-packed coffee shop in Brooklyn can attest.

Spacious recognized these complementary needs and used technology to match the empty restaurants with the hungry coworkers, much as Airbnb matches travelers with unused rooms and other living spaces. Some of the most brilliant ideas in PropTech are simple at their core, and interfaces such as the functional one Spacious built make the process painless. How, you wonder, did no one think of this before, although an incredible amount of work occurs under the hood to make the system sing?

Zenreach helps businesses set up free guest Wi-Fi systems that can also track store visitors and their demographics and create marketing campaigns tailored to each customer. The idea is to build loyalty as well as revenue, and to convert first-timers into repeat customers. Retailers use the platform to build a detailed marketing database that tracks a customer's e-mail, age, number of visits, amount purchased, date of last visit, and so on. The "walk-through rate" (the number of customers who respond to marketing messages by actually walking through the store) is one of the most important metrics and indicators of return on investment, according to Zenreach.

The system can point customers to review sites and social media to build its reputation online too. Retailers see up to a 10 percent increase in positive customer ratings within thirty days, according to Zenreach, which also claims that its customer data collection is five times faster than traditional methods, resulting in 65 percent faster business growth.

Retail, as we pointed out in chapter 1, faces enormous challenges as stores close and online shopping grows. Despite the meteoric rise of e-commerce, however, according to the latest US Census data, around 90 percent of retail purchases still happen in brick-and-mortar stores.[69] Physical retail space is far from dead. The dynamics of online sales are dramatically changing it, though, and retailers out of touch with technology will have trouble surviving in the growing world of virtual dressing rooms, digital tags, beacon technology, and personalized marketing.

Profiting from PropTech

"The reports of my death are greatly exaggerated," Mark Twain famously quipped after rumors of his demise spread. The same tagline might be affixed to brick-and-mortar retail, traditional office space, the conventional residential brokerage, etc. It is easy, amid the excitement generated by real estate technology and emerging innovations, to write premature obituaries. "Disruption" at some point became PropTech's favorite word, but even we, the funders and nurturers of putative disruptors, believe it is overused.

Real estate is transforming, and it is transforming quickly, but as our sampling of start-ups shows, most PropTech companies are providing solutions for the industry: platforms, tools, and services that will improve it, not burn it to the ground. Zillow was painted as a replacement for real estate brokerages, but a dozen years after it was founded, most of the company's money comes from sales agents. Disappearing them, at least at this point, would not seem to be in Zillow's best interest. CompStak, as now configured, could not exist without commercial brokers. Zenreach, Hointer, and a host of other start-ups were designed to enhance the brick-and-mortar retail

---

69   "Quarterly Retail E-Commerce Sales: 3rd Quarter 20180," US Census Bureau News, accessed August 30, 2018, https://www.census.gov/retail/mrts/www/data/pdf/ec_current.pdf.

experience and make it more competitive with e-commerce, often by stealing the best elements of online shopping.

Real estate is transforming with the aid of technology. That much is clear. Whatever niche you're in, it's likely to look very different in a few years. Engaging with the best and most innovative technology is a way to fend off the obituaries because, while some are premature, there will be plenty of death notices. The PropTech space is growing by the hour, and it will necessarily be littered with failures as well as successes. How can you tell what's best for your organization? How do you gain enough insight to choose the tools, platforms, apps with the best return on investment?

It all starts with understanding the fundamentals of real estate technology, especially early-stage real estate tech, and so, in the next chapter, we will roll up our sleeves and take a serious look under the PropTech hood.

INNOVATION CONVERSATION

Michael Rudin, senior vice president, Rudin Management

MetaProp: Rudin Management created a PropTech company called Prescriptive Data to develop Nantum, which includes a building operating system and a system for tenants. How widely are you using it?

Michael Rudin: It's running across our commercial portfolio right now and in a number of non-Rudin properties as well. The tenant fractal is also operational with a couple of our tenants. Dock72 [at the Brooklyn Navy Yard] will be the first building that has our new tenant experience app for individuals too.

MetaProp: Do you have any numbers on how much money you have saved using the system?

Michael Rudin: On average, across our portfolio, we're saving about fifty cents per square foot on operating expenses, so across ten million square feet, that's $5 million a year, give or take. In New York City we started benchmarking in 2005. Since then, our total electric consumption has gone down by 24 percent. On the base building stuff we control—chillers, elevators, mechanical systems—electric consumption has been reduced by 41 percent. It's lower overall because tenant use has actually increased by 11 percent over that time period. As we get more of our tenants to use the tenant fractal, we're hopeful we can help them decrease their electric consumption too. We've reduced our steam consumption by 47 percent over 2005, and we've reduced our carbon output by 44 percent.

MetaProp: You began investing in other start-ups like Enertiv and Radiator Labs after developing Nantum. Why?

Michael Rudin: After Nantum, we said, "Let's leverage our portfolio and our collective expertise, identify things relevant to our business, and become strategic investors where we see a good fit." Radiator Labs was our second investment. It seemed useful for the buildings that we have steam radiators in. Enertiv was complementary to Nantum and our focus on energy efficiency.

MetaProp: What advice would you give to fellow real estate practitioners who are new to the world of PropTech?

Michael Rudin: It's not as easy as identifying a technology and implementing it. A lot of these venture funds go to start-ups and say, "We have all these great real estate LPs [limited partners]. If we invest, they're all going to implement your product." In reality, though, it's not always so simple. We've run the gamut from things that you snap your fingers and they're implemented to things that take multiple years to implement. Ultimately, it's patience and a willingness to listen to the people who are on the ground and using it ... It's not about change for the sake of change, but for the sake of being better at our business and delivering a better experience for our clients ... Be proactive. If you think, *This is something that I would want as a tenant,* try and implement it so that you can offer it to customers. Having an open mind and being patient are key.

CHAPTER FOUR

Defining and Exploring PropTech

"Technology is at the core of pretty much everything we do now on a day-to-day basis, so I can only see it as being hugely detrimental if real estate is left behind. The fact that major companies and chief executives across the world are desperately trying to get their heads around tech is a sign of the times. So, too, is the fact that it is taking many companies so long to actually adopt."

—Emily Wright, tech editor of London-based EG

Categorizing PropTech start-ups is difficult in today's dynamic, rapidly developing space, but a wide variety of useful, evolving taxonomies exist. MetaProp categorizes PropTech by tech, asset type, and geography. Our most useful and unique taxonomy relies on a company's place in the real estate value chain.

––––––––––––

What kind of a business is Zillow?

It seems to be a simple enough question, and if you're familiar with the PropTech giant, your first answer might be something such as "a real estate listing service." The Seattle-based company has a database of more than 110 million homes, including homes for sale, homes for rent, and off-market properties.[70] You're looking for a house, condo, apartment? Enter your parameters at Zillow.com and up pop relevant listings. At first glance, Zillow looks simply like a consumer-facing business that helps people find, sell, and price homes, a search engine for housing.

If you work in real estate, however, you're probably aware that Zillow makes most of its money from real estate agents, as a lead generator, sending them considerable business through its Premier Agent program. To complicate matters further, Zillow calls itself a media company. That claim often raises eyebrows, but as many media companies do, Zillow generates revenue primarily by selling advertising, and it partners with newspapers across the country, trading its online tools for their open-house and classified information.

At MetaProp, we sometimes classify Zillow as consumer-broker tech, since it serves both audiences, but if that label is accurate today, we fully acknowledge that it might not be adequate a few years from now. Zillow's "Instant Offers" program, which allows it to buy homes with or without the involvement of an agent, and its purchase of a mortgage brokerage, move it closer to the transaction, as we noted in chapter 1. By becoming an owner/flipper of real estate in the iBuyer

––––––––––––

70   "About Us," Zillow, accessed January 2019, https://www.zillow.com/corp/About.htm.

space, which could, theoretically, remove agents from the equation, Zillow has muddied the waters even further. How much of the company's business down the road might involve buying and selling property directly, or supplying financial services? To what degree is Zillow moving, as Mike DelPrete suggested, from search engine to service engine?

As many PropTech companies do, Zillow continues to evolve and to resist classification. Classifying and defining are important. They serve an intrinsic human need to make sense of the world, and that need is never stronger than when classifying is a challenge, when change is rapid, categories elusive, and boundaries blurred.

Welcome to the PropTech universe.

As we noted in previous chapters, real estate technology has roots reaching back to the '80s and beyond, but very little of this world existed a decade ago. Since 2012, the growth has been exponential, and keeping up with what has happened just since 2016 is difficult even for those of us deep in the space. Consider that, in the spring of 2016, start-up researcher Venture Scanner tracked 1,137 PropTech companies, with a combined total funding of $16.99 billion.[71] As of June 2018, the Venture Scanner was tracking 1,659 PropTech companies representing $55 billion in total funding.[72]

How can you hope to make sense of a universe in which the number of start-ups has grown by 46 percent, according to Venture Scanner's numbers, and investment has risen by more than 220 percent in just two years? Unless keeping up with PropTech is your full-time job, you can't. You need help tracking this tidal wave of tech-powered innovation. In chapter 5, we will highlight some of

---

71 "Venture Investing in Real Estate Technology—Q3 2017," Venture Scanner, accessed September 9, 2018, https://www.venturescanner.com/blog/tags/proptech%20report.
72 "Mid-Year Real Estate Technology Exits Analysis," Venture Scanner, accessed September 9, 2018, https://www.venturescanner.com/blog/tags/proptech.

the advisors, events, blogs, news sources, associations, academic programs, accelerators, and other resources that make navigating these constantly churning waters easier. In this chapter, we will help you define and categorize PropTech, so that you can explore it within a framework that brings some order to the chaos and makes it all more digestible.

The first point of any PropTech primer has to be that there are now nearly as many taxonomies for real estate technology as there are analysts tracking the space. None of them is right or wrong and all are evolving, but if you hope to engage with real estate technology, you need a map, and maybe several, to guide you. On the corporate side, viewing the space through an organizational lens helps you find and track relevant solutions, locate useful partners more quickly—which can improve ROI—locate your start-up in the market, assess the competition, and find business. Moreover, investing in PropTech without a working schema would be as naïve as buying into mutual funds without knowing the difference between fixed-income, equity, index, and other varieties.

Knowing the opportunities and threats posed by PropTech can boost the bottom line for real estate firms, and that knowledge is much more useful when placed in logical, manageable buckets.

With apologies to Francis Bacon once again, knowledge is money, not just power. We hope we have made the point that knowing the opportunities and threats posed by PropTech can boost the bottom line for real estate firms, and that knowledge is much more useful when placed in logical, manageable buckets.

If, as we argued above, the taxonomy that's toughest to create is the one most needed, classifying early-stage PropTech is the highest priority. Early-stage is the newest and most innovative part of the space. It contains the freshest entrepreneurs, the latest start-ups, the newest tech, the greatest risk, and the greatest potential return. Later-stage PropTech is today's technology waiting to scale. Early-stage PropTech is tomorrow's technology waiting to be proven. It is the most rapidly changing segment of the market, and thus, the hardest to fully grasp.

It is also our specialty. Everything we do at MetaProp feeds into our analysis of this part of the space, which we track with great effort and humility. We leverage our advising activities and partnerships with industry, our accelerator and relationships with start-ups, our involvement in academia, and our venture capital fund and investor connections in order to understand early-stage PropTech from all angles, and to share our expertise with a variety of stakeholders. Because it is both the least understood part of the space and what we know best, we will pay particular attention to early-stage PropTech here and in the remaining chapters.

Our own PropTech taxonomy is informed by these diverse relationships with industry, start-ups, and investors, as well as our backgrounds in real estate and tech. Our classification is unique and, we think, extremely useful. We will present it here alongside several others, with the caveat that it, too, continues to evolve. PropTech is dynamic and growing at a dizzying pace. Most of the definitions and classifications out there are useful in some way, but those presenting their model as static or monolithic are, at best, naïve.

Evolving Definitions

Before we discuss the many ways of parsing PropTech, we should begin by saying that there is wide and healthy disagreement about not just how to define PropTech but even what it should be called. In chapter 1, we pointed out that while some prefer other labels, including real estate tech, RETech, RealTech, or CREtech (commercial real estate technology), beginning in 2016, we at MetaProp began promulgating the name PropTech, which is sometimes heard in Europe, to reflect the increasingly global nature of the movement.

Since then, the label of PropTech has been widely recognized in the US, though RETech and others are still common. The question of how to define PropTech is a little more complex. In chapter 1, we offered a version of this basic definition:

> PropTech, short for "property technology," refers to the software, tools, platforms, apps, websites, and other digital solutions enlisted by real estate practitioners, from architects to construction managers to brokers. It realizes efficiencies and provides innovation to facilitate real estate activities, including designing, developing, building, buying, selling, leasing, managing, appraising, financing, marketing, investing, and so on.

This book is designed to be useful for those new to PropTech, so we have tried to keep our definition concrete and grounded. Websites or apps that help consumers search for homes or apartments are PropTech. So are the platforms that help general contractors manage construction, or that aid commercial brokers in finding and analyzing comps. Other PropTech innovations help developers select sites, landlords lease space, property managers run buildings, and asset managers analyze portfolios.

Our good friend, gadfly, and noted PropTech expert James Dearsley teamed up with Professor Andrew Baum to craft a slightly more abstract definition:

> PropTech is one small part of the wider digital transformation of the property industry. It describes a movement driving a mentality change within the real estate industry and its consumers regarding technology-driven innovation in the data assembly, transaction, and design of buildings and cities.

This is a little more academic perhaps, but there are a number of things we like here. First, Dearsley and Baum put PropTech in a larger context, the "wider digital transformation," which in chapter 1 we referred to as the fourth industrial revolution. Many of the technological innovations unveiled in real estate today are coming from within the industry or have been designed specifically for it. Increasingly, however, outside advances ranging from autonomous vehicles to robotics will precipitate changes in the way real estate works.

Second, we very much like Dearsley and Baum's emphasis on a change in mentality. When they first dip their toes in the PropTech pool, many observers, including high-level real estate professionals, see only the tech in PropTech. They think of it in terms of helpful new tools—a powerful platform, advanced sensors, and killer CRM— or in terms of emerging technologies, such as IoT, artificial intelligence, virtual reality, 3-D printing, etc.

Think of tech, then, as a catalyst and a means to an end—

Think of tech, then, as a catalyst and a means to an end—the end being greater profit—with PropTech innovation as the path that increased wealth.

the end being greater profit—with PropTech innovation as the path that increased wealth.

Exploring Taxonomies

If defining PropTech remains tricky, devising a workable taxonomy is even trickier. As we pointed out in chapter 3, this is a brave new real estate world, and all of us, the authors of this book included, are still figuring out the landscape. To some extent, we always will be. Inspiration is the soul of innovation, but change is its only constant. The world of real estate technology is thrilling today partly because it is advancing so rapidly. How we at MetaProp categorize PropTech has evolved during the last few years and will continue to do so as the contours of the space shift and develop.

In "PropTech 3.0: The Future of Real Estate," Andrew Baum presents a Venn diagram that makes for a good organizational starting point because it gives a broad birds-eye view of PropTech.

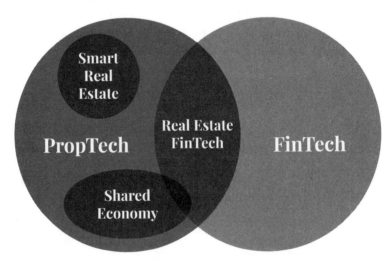

Andrew Baum, "PropTech 3.0: The Future of Real Estate," University of Oxford, SAID Business School, April 2017, http://eureka.sbs.ox.ac.uk/6485/1/ 122037%20PropTech_FINAL.pdf.

FinTech is closely related to PropTech and has been a catalyst for tech solutions in the real estate industry. This has occurred partly because consumers long used to banking by phone and buying stocks through their e-trade app want to interact with real estate in more convenient ways, and partly because FinTech has so many natural intersections with real estate. Baum's Venn diagram demonstrates this with a large overlap between FinTech and PropTech, an area he calls in his book "real estate FinTech." This includes lending of various kinds, insurance, financing, payment platforms, and more.

Baum's other two subsectors of PropTech are smart real estate and the shared economy. Smart real estate can include everything from a parking garage to an entire city, but primarily refers to buildings using sensors, automation, and sophisticated platforms for everything from security to maintenance to energy usage. Sustainability is a key driver here. The shared (or sharing, or collaboration) economy refers to platforms and tools that allow for utilization and monetization of underused assets—for example, the extra space let through Airbnb, or the restaurant that Spacious turns into coworking space during off-hours.

MetaProp's Taxonomies

BY TECH

At MetaProp, one of the first ways in which we classified PropTech was by type of technology. Our broad categories here are software, hardware, and tech-enabled service. Software, of course, refers to the programs used to operate computers and other devices, but more specifically, we are talking about software as a service (SaaS). In this cloud-computing distribution model, common in PropTech, a provider hosts applications and makes them available to customers via the internet. CompStak's platform for exchanging information about comps, which we explored earlier, is an example, as are the applications built by HotelTonight and Travtus, noted in previous chapters.

Hardware refers to physical components, including handheld devices, sensors, cameras, displays, and so on. The IoT has a large hardware contingent, including sensors and regulators. Tech-enabled services include companies such as Bowery, which provides appraisals, an age-old real estate service, but with a cloud-based mobile inspection app that improves the process. Compass sales agents similarly provide a familiar type of service for those buying and selling homes, but they rely on new tech tools to deliver it.

This tech taxonomy has the advantage of consistent categories and thoroughness. Everything in the PropTech universe fits in one of these buckets, each of which designates a type of technology. We still find this classification useful, but the categories are quite broad and involve significant overlap. Nearly every piece of PropTech hardware also uses software, for example, and tech-enabled services often use both.

BY ASSET TYPE

Another, more detailed taxonomy that we use is division by asset type. Is the PropTech company solving a problem for office buildings, retail, industrial, single-family, multifamily, hospitality? Which asset type is the solution geared toward, and what is the interplay, if any, between the primary asset type and any secondary asset type served? Here, too, there is overlap, since things that are useful for offices, for example, frequently are also useful for multifamily. Considering how innovations are being utilized by asset type is an important way of looking at real estate technologies. It highlights the depth and state of the market for a given solution, as well as distribution.

BY GEOGRAPHY

A third, increasingly important way in which we categorize PropTech is by geography. *Location, location, location* has forever been the mantra in real estate. At MetaProp, we altered this motto slightly with our tagline: *location, location, innovation.* Our point there is to highlight the primacy of location and its connection to tech. What works for real estate in New York doesn't necessarily work in San Francisco, and what flies in Beijing might not in Moscow. PropTech has become a global phenomenon, as we pointed out in chapter 1, but real estate remains a hyper-local and highly regulated commodity. Think of New York's unique rules regarding cooperatives, Europe's high standards for sustainability, and the patchwork of regulations affecting Airbnb in locations around the world.

BY REAL ESTATE VALUE CHAIN

Finally, the most important, useful, and unique way in which we classify PropTech is through its place in the real estate value chain. People, typically, think of the value chain model in terms of products. A company procures raw materials and through a series of processes adds value to them by manufacturing, marketing, postsale servicing, and so on.

THE REAL ESTATE VALUE CHAIN: DIRT → DISPOSITION			
Analysis & Financing	**Space Identification + Listing**	**Site Selection & Negotiation**	**Diligence**
• Zoning	• Marketplace	• Brokerage	• Prospecting
• Appraisal	• O2O	• Tour	• Title
• Budgeting	• Marketing	• Comps	• Econometrics
• Modeling	• Review		• Risk pricing

We use the same principle for real estate, considering every step in its lifecycle, "from dirt to disposition." Consider a new office tower. Long before a shovel hits dirt, a detailed analysis is done to assess the market and the size and type of tower likely to succeed. Financing must be found, a site located and purchased, plans drawn, and a building constructed. Later, that building will have to be marketed, leased, managed, and maintained. Rents will be collected, bills paid, security monitored, etc.

We have skipped an enormous number of steps in the process, but you get the idea. MetaProp categorizes PropTech companies by which step their solution works for—namely, where they fall in the real estate value chain. One advantage and challenge of this unique taxonomy is that it's flexible, with an infinite number of possible buckets. If it suited your purposes, you might limit this schema to three steps—design, construction, and marketing, say—or, just as easily, three hundred.

Here are the buckets we use in our value-chain taxonomy:

1. analysis and financing

2. space ID and listing

3. site selection and negotiation

THE REAL ESTATE VALUE CHAIN: DIRT → DISPOSITION			
Development + Construction	**Process Automation**	**Space Usage & Management**	**Payments + Services**
• Project oversight • Architecture • Design • Engineering • Compliance • Construction	• Sales • Leasing • Underwriting • Broker tools	• "Basement Tech" • HVAC • Facilities management • Security	• Rental • Utilities • Service providers • Trade • Credit

4. diligence

5. development and construction

6. process automation

7. space usage and management

8. payments and services

Real estate is a massive, diverse asset, but we have found that these categories capture the lifecycle well, allowing us to locate where the start-ups we're looking at, investing in, mentoring, and so on, sit in the value chain. This taxonomy emphasizes both exactly where a start-up is adding value (the foundation of any value-chain model) and where it's earning revenue. It reveals connections between start-ups, which might have complementary or sequential functions, and it can highlight trends and opportunities. Does a small number of start-ups in the site selection and negotiation bucket point to unsolved problems and opportunities for innovation? How might a company in management interact with another in payment and services?

At its most basic level, this taxonomy also emphasizes the function of a start-up or product, not what's under the hood, a distinction that can be vital for leaders who understand real estate, but tech, not so much. In an interview with us, Emily Wright, tech editor of London-based EG and one of the world's leading PropTech journalists, said her greatest challenge in helping readers understand that PropTech involves:

> … the difference between knowing what the technology is and what it does. People rarely need to know what a system, software, or platform actually is—and by that I mean how it is put together and its inner workings. It is all about knowing what it does, and jargon has scared off potential adopters and converts. If any of us had to get our heads around the inner workings of our mobile phones before actually using them, very few of us would have one.

Using the real estate value chain as our primary taxonomy feels organic partly because this is how real estate practitioners view their own businesses. If our backgrounds were only in tech or investing, we might never have arrived here, but as two people whose careers also have been steeped in real estate, we immediately felt that this model was the right one when we hit on it.

This is not to say that this taxonomy is perfect or complete. As is everything in PropTech, our model is also likely to evolve and change with the space. Deciding on the number and nature of the buckets involves more art than science. Real estate is such a gargantuan asset that a single subcategory within one of our buckets above might be worth a trillion dollars. Additional distinct categories will likely emerge as the market matures and specialties develop. For instance, we now include ConTech, which is still very much at an early stage, as a subset of PropTech. When the field grows large enough, however, we might consider it a separate category.

Our categorization of construction technology, of course, is the exact opposite of that of Baum, who currently separates ConTech from PropTech but says he might later make it a subset. Neither view is right or wrong, any more than a particular lens is the right one for a camera. For some purposes you want a telephoto, and at other times, the wide-angle lens does the trick.

PropTech is too dynamic to be framed in steel. Attempting to lock down categories as the space evolves, we think, would be a mistake. Much better to let the market decide the boundaries and to alter them when innovation or the forces of supply and demand warrant. Through our roles as advisors, investors, mentors, and partners, we are in close contact with enterprise CEOs, start-up entrepreneurs, venture capitalists, academics, and other stakeholders. Those diverse touchpoints in the world of PropTech allow us to revise our definitions in real time and move the lines as the space changes.

As many readers no doubt know, another common way to classify start-ups, which we haven't even broached, is according to their stage of development. This is, typically, carved up in terms of capital investment, with an early "seed phase" followed by funding rounds labelled A, B, C, and so on. We'll explore how this system functions in PropTech in chapter 7, on investment.

Assessing start-ups is most difficult from conception through the earliest funding rounds, when a product or service is still being tested, a team formed, and a potential market plumbed. We might think of this as "the idea stage," and again, it's our forte at MetaProp. As with choosing the optimal buckets for a taxonomy based on the real estate value chain, analyzing start-ups that don't yet have a track record or a fully fleshed-out product is more art than science. We will explore more ways of considering and classifying these early-stage start-ups and share some of our tricks of the trade in the next chapter, "Start-Up Strategies for Engaging with Industry."

INNOVATION CONVERSATION

Michael Beckerman, founder and CEO, CREtech

MetaProp: What are your day-to-day responsibilities in your organization?

Michael Beckerman: I run CRETech.com, the largest platform devoted to commercial real estate tech. It's a twelve-person organization devoted to connecting the commercial real estate and tech sectors. Our site focuses on events, data/research, aggregated news, and advisory services. My day-to-day usually revolves around speaking at conferences, connecting with VC's and investors, hearing from start-ups and learning about their products as well as strategizing with landlords and brokers on their tech strategies.

My company also owns two other sites that are scaling well in the market: The News Funnel, a curated news site for commercial real estate, and The Content Funnel, which provides content marketing services, also for commercial real estate professionals. Both have incredibly strong leadership, so I spend most of my time managing the CRETech platform.

MetaProp: How did you become interested in PropTech and innovation?

Michael Beckerman: I previously spent twenty-five years building the largest public relations firm that specialized in CRE. Around 2008, I had a gut feeling that tech was going to impact CRE, and to quote Wayne Gretzky, I went "to where the puck is headed" and put a plan in motion to sell my interests in the firm I built and enter the CRETech sector, which I did full time in 2011.

MetaProp: In the next ten years, what area of the real estate industry do you think will change the most dramatically?

Michael Beckerman: There are three areas that I think will be the most impacted. One, AI and predictive analytics will be transformative, providing professionals with more actionable data than at any time in history. Previously, the entire sector operated on historical data. That will all change with AI. Second, I think that space as a service will completely upend the way office and multi-family assets will be managed and built. Along with that, short-term leases will impact everything from underwriting to architecture/space design. Third, I think there is a coming revolution in space visualization that few are talking about. Beyond VR [virtual reality], holography and AR [augmented reality] will usher in an exciting revolution in the way space is planned, designed, built, leased, marketed, and furnished.

MetaProp: What is the most important innovation and technology-driven initiative in your organization today?

Michael Beckerman: We are building the largest data library in CRETech, which will be the single source for professionals to discover all things commercial real estate tech.

MetaProp: What is one interesting thing about you that most people don't already know?

Michael Beckerman: I am the least tech person, personally.

MetaProp: Assess the pace of innovation in the real estate industry and how it is evolving.

Michael Beckerman: Investment is profoundly ahead of adoption in the sector. What surprises me every day is the unwillingness of people to embrace change. Just as Airbnb disrupted hotels and few saw that coming, Uber did the same to the taxi industry, WeWork to the flex-space sector and Amazon to retail, change is coming to CRE. Unfortunately, those that ignore it will be like a deer in headlights.

CHAPTER FIVE

Start-Up Strategies for Engaging with Industry

"Don't be afraid to share the company with others who can help you build it. A lot of people who have an idea feel like it's precious and it's theirs, but there's no way to build an enduring company as a single person. It's very important to consistently find partners and people who can buy into your vision and help you build it, and you have to share the upside with those other talented people."

—**Preston Pesek,** cofounder of Spacious

"By far the most important step, which is actually a continuous process, is to talk with customers and potential customers to understand what they deal with on a daily basis. There is no amount of planning or development that can replace feeling the pain points

that your customers are feeling. When you have that part down, the business plans, pitches, sales, funding, etc. all fall into place."

—Connell McGill, Enertiv

We encourage start-ups to take a minimum-viable-product (MVP) approach as they grow: fail fast and iterate often. Engaging with industry through pilots, partnerships, and investment is vital, but cultural differences and other obstacles make these relationships complex. MetaProp has developed strategies and resources to bridge the gaps.

Blank stares and raised eyebrows greeted Ryan Simonetti nine years ago when he pitched Convene, his start-up concept, to commercial real estate companies. Simonetti's background was in hotel and office investing, and he wanted to combine elements of those two asset types. Why couldn't an office building offer the services of a lifestyle hotel, he wondered, with the same high level of design, meeting space, technology, food, beverage, and other amenities? Simonetti's gut said tenants would love a building offering this kind of experience. Their workers would be happier and more productive, and the companies themselves would get better service without having to build out and maintain the amenities space. Demand for such offices would rise, he reasoned, as would rents, which would make the buildings more valuable.

Simonetti's plan was to partner directly with owners to create common amenities in their buildings, but first, he had to convince them that his idea was worth pursuing.

"They thought we were crazy," Simonetti told us in an interview. "If I'm a building owner, why would I build a shared-amenity infrastructure that tenants could use on demand, as opposed to having them sign a lease, take space, and build it out on their own? Why would I agree to take some of my leasable real estate out of what I could sell to a corporation and turn it into this amenity?"

After a skeptical response, Simonetti and his partner, Chris Kelly, rolled out one basic product to start, and then layered on services gradually, spending the next five years trying to engage industry partners.

Today, Convene has tech-enabled meeting, event, and flexible workspaces in five cities, with more in the works. Its industry partners include the likes of Brookfield, the Durst Organization, and RXR Realty, and in mid-2018, the company closed $152 million in series D financing, bringing its total equity funding to $260 million. That recent funding round will help it launch Elevate, a digital interface now in beta testing in several buildings. The platform will allow tenants and their workers to interact with building services, amenities, and infrastructure through their phones.

Convene made it.

Most early-stage start-ups do not. No one knows better than we do at MetaProp that having a good idea is not enough. Assessing the needs of the market, tailoring a service or product to those needs, gaining access to capital, scaling in the right way, and finding distribution are vital parts of the equation. *Equation* is probably the wrong word, since these elements involve more art than science. Zach, as we've mentioned, teaches courses on PropTech at Columbia University, including one geared toward aspiring entrepreneurs, but he is the first to admit that every start-up is different; there is no single, predetermined route from idea to acquisition or IPO.

STARTUP FAILURE

Up to 75 percent of startups fail. Why?

- can't raise enough initial angel/VC funding

- wasting too much money at early stages

- company doesn't begin with the best people

- doesn't produce something people want

- hires too many people too quickly

- hires the wrong people, or people with the wrong skills

- doesn't produce a working product in a timely manner

- not able to successfully monetize the idea

- beaten out by a competitor

From Marty Stepp. Some ideas and content from Wayne Yamamoto.

The start-up's journey—and at MetaProp we very much think of it as a journey—is full of detours, false starts, and revisions. In our assessments of hundreds of early-stage PropTech start-ups, however, we have determined that success tends to involve these three ingredients: partnership, investment, and community. Engagement with industry, the enormous challenge Ryan Simonetti faced as he launched Convene, is vital for all three, and often is the difference between growth and stagnation.

Through our accelerator (which we'll explain shortly), investments, advising, mentoring, events, networking, and other activities, MetaProp acts as a bridge between start-ups and industry. We enlist every part of our business to ease the kind of friction that Convene felt nearly a decade ago as it attempted to win over landlords. In this chapter, we'll share some of what we've learned about the ways that successful start-ups engage with industry to understand market needs, access capital, develop and test products, scale strategically, and find distribution.

Hipster, Hacker, Hustler

Most readers know what we mean by a start-up, but definitions can vary, so we'll begin with ours: *a company, partnership, or temporary organization designed to search for a repeatable and scalable business model.* Start-ups are often poised for rapid growth and rooted in technology, and early-stage start-ups in particular tend to offer high risk and high reward.

As we've seen, start-ups are often characterized as "disruptors" that restructure markets, or create new ones. Disruption is real, but as we hope our many examples have shown, most PropTech start-ups are formed to provide solutions for industry—faster transactions, smoother processes, better information—not to upend it. Change tends to happen more incrementally than the hype implies, and one challenge for many PropTech start-ups is convincing incumbents that a new solution can provide a competitive edge.

Start-up founders come from all walks, but tend to fit into one of three categories:

1. **Technologist.** This is a common PropTech profile on the West Coast. A software whiz or someone with deep technical know-how sees a better way to provide a product or service in real estate, often while buying a home, renting an apartment, browsing office space, and so on. Patrick Burns, cofounder of Spruce, a title company that offers

digital closings, fits this bill. He studied statistics and then, as a research assistant, focused on their application in data analysis, machine learning, and other realms. An obsession with the mechanics of the real estate transaction became his entrée into PropTech.

2. **Entrepreneur.** As with technologists, many entrepreneurs enter PropTech after a less than optimal personal experience with real estate. The business mind quickly arrives at a better model and dives in. For Susannah Vila, this scenario played out after she signed a year-long lease while in business school at Columbia. Circumstances forced her to sublet the space, but finding a tenant to take over her lease, qualifying that person, and coordinating with the landlord was a nightmare. She began working on a solution as part of a class project and wound up creating Flip, a platform that matches tenants and subletters, performs credit checks, and coordinates with landlords. First-time founders tend to take longer to develop than serial entrepreneurs do, and they make more mistakes, but often, they think so far outside the box that they create a blockbuster company. Serial entrepreneurs can scale quickly. For them, it's lather, rinse, repeat. However, they have a fair number of flops too.

3. **Real estate practitioner.** Professionals from within the industry often see problems up close and think of ways to build a better mousetrap. Ryan Simonetti, cofounder of Convene, falls into this category. His years of managing investments in hotel and office space led him to the hybrid concept behind his start-up. The real estate insider has the

advantage of knowing the terrain, though as we saw with Simonetti's example, getting industry players to accept a good idea can still be a challenge.

Wherever the idea for a start-up begins, assembling the right team is critical for the early-stage organization. In fact, Zak Schwarzman, the MetaProp partner who leads our venture capital funds, argues that of the three big factors he's always assessing in early-stage PropTech—people, product, and market—*people is the most important variable*. We'll delve into this idea with Zak's help in chapter 7 on investment. Here, we simply want to dispel the notion that a great idea carries the day. As investors and mentors, we pass over dozens of great ideas every month because the team doesn't seem right or ready. An idea can be developed, a product refined, but if the team lacks fundamentals, course correction becomes difficult.

An idea can be developed, a product refined, but if the team lacks fundamentals, course correction becomes difficult.

What should a solid team look like? We often quote Rei Inamoto, the former chief creative officer for digital agency AKQA, who posits that a successful team needs "a hipster, a hacker, and a hustler." The hipster, in Inamoto's formulation, is the creative force, often on board as a designer. The hacker is the technical prodigy who can work wonders with code, and the hustler is the one who understands the business case and can convey it, keeping everyone focused on customer needs.

We don't subscribe to any rigid team formula, not even one as fun as Inamoto's. However, we do look for talents, skill sets, and personalities that complement each other in an early-stage start-up. Is there someone who understands the technology at a deep level and can address the technical challenges? Is there someone focused on the actual market need who can convincingly pitch the solution? Are the personalities and egos compatible?

Early-Stage Start-Up Development

Some would-be PropTech entrepreneurs think that they need to perfect their product or service before approaching players in the real estate industry. This was once a common model for development and still occurs in some cases. This, for example, was how Siri, Apple's virtual assistant, was born at the Stanford Research Institute. Powered by the deep pockets of private equity firm Warburg Pincus, many PhDs, and the resources of the SRI International Artificial Intelligence Center, the effort took shape over years, behind closed doors before, and voilà, Siri was loosed on the world.

For the early-stage start-ups with a lab full of Stanford PhDs and tens of millions from the get-go, this is a possible model. For the rest—namely, everyone we deal with—we encourage an MVP approach. The term was coined by Frank Robinson, president and cofounder of SyncDev, but popularized by Eric Ries, author of *The Lean Start-up*, and Steve Blank, author of *The Start-up Owner's Manual* and the seminal book, *The Four Steps to the Epiphany*.

The idea is to get a basic version of a product in the hands of customers as quickly as possible in order to get feedback, understand mistakes, return to the drawing board, and get the next, improved version out so that you can get feedback, understand mistakes, return to the drawing board, and … you get the idea. Failing fast and iterating often, making incremental improvements based on an almost continuous feedback loop, allows agile entrepreneurs to do incredible things with limited resources, as we see firsthand all the time.

This philosophy is perhaps best summed up by the now famous words of Reid Hoffman, the founder of LinkedIn: "If you are not embarrassed by the first version of your product, you've launched too late."[73]

Start-up Commons, which provides education and training for start-ups, as well as consulting and other services, produced the helpful diagram below, outlining phases of start-up development.[74]

STARTUP FINANCING CYCLE

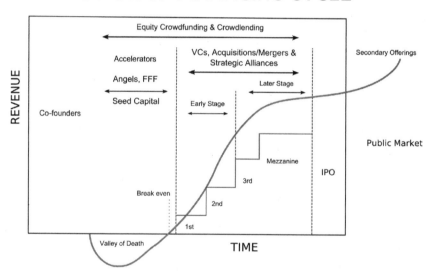

Wikipedia, s.v. "Startup company," accessed January 2019, https://commons. wikimedia.org/wiki/File:Startup_financing_cycle.svg.

The process is perhaps messier and less linear than any graphic can convey, but this one provides a good overview of the typical

73   Nick Saint, "If You're Not Embarrassed by the First Version of Your Product, You've Launched Too Late," Business Insider, November 13, 2009, https://www.businessinsider. com/the-iterate-fast-and-release-often-philosophy-of-entrepreneurship-2009-11.
74   "Startup Development Phases," Startup Commons, accessed September 15, 2018, https:// www.startupcommons.org/startup-development-phases.html.

early-stage start-up's journey in PropTech. The first phases, as we've discussed, involve coming up with a scalable idea and forming a team with complementary skill sets. The solution has to fit a real problem and serve a large enough target market to be financially viable. This, according to Simonetti, does not necessarily mean planning the next Amazon, "There are many problems, even small ones, that entrepreneurs could solve through new ways of doing things and build amazing businesses," Simonetti told us, pointing out that addressing even a small problem in an industry as large as real estate can be highly profitable. "Those might be lifestyle businesses or really big scalable businesses ... The problems are almost endless."

Consider the Cozy, the smart radiator enclosure we mentioned in chapter 3. As a start-up, Radiator Labs chose a small, specific problem—old radiators' inefficiency and lack of control—and delivered a tech solution that might be deployed in tens of thousands of buildings just in New York City. Susannah Vila, of subletting platform Flip, chose another small problem (though one that feels enormous when it's yours) with a massive market. Close to 70 percent of New Yorkers rent, so Flip's potential customer base in that city alone numbers in the millions.

Tackling bigger problems means bigger market potential for early-stage start-ups, but it's also, usually, a solution that takes more time and money to implement. After finding a problem with enough market share, and devising a possible solution in the formation phase of development, start-ups validate the minimum viable product, tailoring it to customer needs through testing and piloting. Partnerships with industry players, the first element of success in our tripartite formula, are vital here.

Growing with Industry Partners[75]

Enertiv, a PropTech company that digitalizes building infrastructure to streamline operations and maintenance, says that it reduces operating expenses by 7 percent, on average, as we noted in chapter 3, creating roughly twelve dollars per square foot of asset value. Getting to that math required years of partnership with owner-operators who gave regular feedback and supplied millions of hours of machine data, which was used to adjust the product. Start-ups often pitch their solutions for use in a single building or a small piece of a portfolio in the hope of getting more business later. More importantly in the early stages, they do this to gain critical data and user response.

In addition to providing test cases and pilots, legacy companies also frequently become a source of critical investment capital for early-stage start-ups. We'll touch on this idea below and explore it in more depth in chapter 7 on investment.

Interacting with those legacy companies is an important part of understanding your market, according to Patrick Burns, cofounder of Spruce, a digital title and escrow company. The testing and research needed to grow a start-up require intense labor and improvisation:

> Wherever you have problems that are very domain-specific, particularly in this [title] world, you kind of have to figure out how things work. There is no manual on how to start a title company … You've got to do the research. You've got to read the statutes. You've got to talk to the person who has been working on that problem for the last twenty years.

---

75   Quotations in this section are from interviews conducted by the authors.

In 2018, two years after launching, Spruce operated in thirty-eight states, each with its own set of laws and regulations regarding title insurance. Navigating that landscape proved just as challenging as building the technology to provide fast, affordable, transparent closings. Part of Spruce's success rests on gradually building partnerships with big traditional title companies such as Fidelity, Chicago Title, WFG, North American, and others through which it underwrites.

Scaling strategically was also critical for Dustin DeVan's business, BuildingConnected, a construction industry platform that connects general contractors, subcontractors, and owners, with built-in mechanisms to qualify subs, send and track bid invitations, and more. DeVan and cofounder Jesse Pedersen took a market-by-market approach, focusing on general contractors. In DeVan's words:

> I think every company will face different challenges in developing their go-to-market strategy. The good thing about BuildingConnected was that we knew we only had to target general contractors, and they were going to bring their subcontractors on board through the bidding process. Now, we have 250,000 businesses on Building-Connected, and that was done just by targeting GCs. We were able to be hyper-selective.

Adoption by industry often takes much longer than early-stage start-ups anticipate. Entrepreneurs' agility in rolling out just one of several products, or a part of one product, adjusting the phase-in schedule, and so on, is key. Again, a good idea guarantees nothing. Convene is finally executing the original design its cofounders shared nearly a decade ago, according to Simonetti, but industry acceptance has only come in the last three years.

"Entrepreneurs have to be mindful of the question, Is the market ready to adopt my idea today, or am I too early?" Simonetti told us. "And the challenge is you don't know until you get started." Convene had to wait for the owners and managers of office towers to catch up to its preferred model. "As the market matured, we started to evolve our offerings to speak to the true vision, but if we'd brought it out too soon, I don't know if we would have been successful."

Start-ups must be patient and persistent, Simonetti cautioned, and must understand that legacy companies are faced with a frightening degree of change management as technology and innovation ramp up.

"With consumers, you create a great app, they download it, and the cost of making that switch is nothing," Simonetti told us. "The cost of picking the wrong solution for Brookfield Property Group or Blackstone or RXR is massive. As entrepreneurs, we have to be empathetic to that."

A lack of clear benchmarks for start-ups can add to corporate discomfort. This occurs in the validation phase, indicated in the "Startup Financing" graphic shown earlier, titled "Initial Key Performance Indicators (KPIs) Identified." Oftentimes, there are no obvious KPIs for innovative start-ups, which unsettles industry partners used to price-per-square-foot, vacancy rates, net operating income, and other standard metrics. This was the case for Spacious, the start-up that we introduced earlier and that turns restaurants into coworking locations by day, when they're normally vacant. As Preston Pesek, Spacious cofounder and CEO, put it:

> When we started, there were no real industry benchmarks
> for how we measure on-site profit and loss. We have our
> own nomenclature for the KPIs and the P&Ls [profit
> and loss, or income, statements] at Spacious. We look

at subscriptions-over-seats as a ratio that we study on a per-location basis, and that's a very different analysis than rent-per-square-foot or hotel ADR [average daily rate], or any of the other common metrics that you find in commercial real estate.

How do potential industry partners value a company, such as Spacious, that has no direct parallel? This is an important part of the role filled by MetaProp and other organizations in the PropTech ecosystem. We serve as translators, helping start-ups and industry answer such questions while fostering the three key elements of successful start-ups: community, investment, and partnership.

Community/Investment Key

We will cover investment in detail in chapter 7. Here, we want to emphasize that it is inextricably linked to community and partnerships. Funding for early-stage PropTech start-ups presents a unique challenge for all of the reasons just mentioned. There often are no clear benchmarks. Valuing an early-stage start-up and assessing its potential is impossible for many investors. Moreover, investors who don't understand the industry or the growing PropTech ecosystem can hamstring or even suffocate innovative entrepreneurs.

This, as we've noted, is a large part of our *raison d'être* at MetaProp. We spend an enormous amount of time evaluating start-ups, gauging their potential, mentoring them, and connecting them with industry partners and investors. Those two groups often overlap. Many large-asset managers and even smaller commercial firms now have investment arms focused on real estate technology. We advise a number of these investors. They want a healthy return, of course, but are often driven by a search for tech solutions that will improve their core businesses. We operate exceptionally well in this zone because we not only have backgrounds deep in real estate and technology but we also have experience as entrepreneurs. Moreover, because we operate our own PropTech venture capital funds, we see the equation from the investors' side every day.

Pesek, who worked in the capital markets before cofounding Spacious, told us that the right investors can play a broad and pivotal role for an early-stage PropTech start-up:

> For a company like Spacious, especially at the earliest stages, there's no data. There's no information about how well it might do, so that's precisely why you want to raise venture capital, as opposed to other kinds of money. You need to sell a significant portion of the equity of your business to someone who understands what it means.

Venture capitalists (VCs), as most readers probably know, specialize in small or emerging companies with high potential and high risk. Typically, they supply funding in return for equity or an ownership stake in the business. The right VC understands the nature of the risk and the unique challenges of developing a business model around tech-based innovation over time.

"[VCs] give you at least some of the resources necessary for building an early-stage team and kind of orienting you in the realm, how you should prepare for the next round of financing," Pesek told us. "They help you with recruiting and introductions. Investors are extraordinarily helpful in the world of early stage."

We'll pick up our discussion of investment in chapter 7, and here, take Pesek's insights as a segue into the Venn diagram below, which we use to illustrate the connections and overlap between partnership, investment, and community.

DURABLE REAL ESTATE FIRMS WILL MOVE TOWARDS TIER-1 INNOVATION STRATEGIES

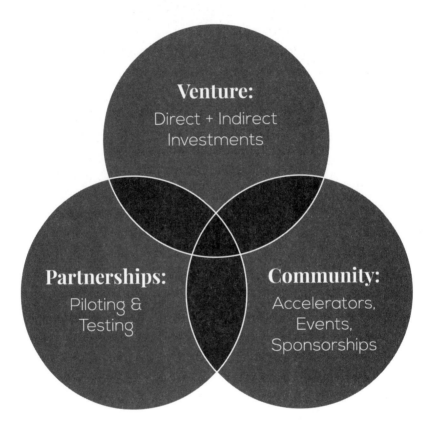

As we've seen, many of the traditional real estate industry players partnering with early-stage start-ups also invest in them, an overlap highlighted in our diagram. What, however, do we mean by *community?* Note that Pesek's comments, which began with investing, quickly moved into mentoring, recruiting, and introductions. These and other elements of community are tightly interwoven with partnerships (including piloting) and investing.

Community is a subject near and dear to our hearts at MetaProp, because if you had to boil the hydra-headed beast that we are down to one word, this would probably be the best choice. All of our endeavors—investing, advising, mentoring, accelerating, event planning, researching, teaching, and so on, are, at bottom, about community. We take pride in this notion because, as almost any source we have quoted in this book would attest, a decade or even seven or eight years ago, there really wasn't a PropTech community. We have worked diligently, as have many extremely smart people and agile organizations, to build one centered here in New York City.

This community includes a growing number of venture-capital funds devoted exclusively or largely to PropTech. It includes advisors and consultants specializing in real estate technology, as well as a proliferation of events, blogs, publications, contests, and associations devoted to PropTech. MetaProp alone organizes, co-produces and/or sponsors more than thirty events each year, including MIPIM PropTech in New York City, Europe, and Asia; the PropTech Leaders Roundtable; Women in PropTech (WiPT); MetaProp Accelerator Demo Days; and New York City Real Estate Tech Week, which has gained a reputation as the Davos of real estate technology.

Other events include the Realcomm CIO Forum series, the MIT World Real Estate Forum, the Bisnow Innovation Summit, CREtech series in San Francisco, New York, and other major markets, Future:PropTech in Europe, Real Estate Innovation Network (REIN) at EXPO REAL in Germany, and many more. One of the biggest annual real estate conferences reflects the increasingly global nature of the real estate tech community. Over four days in Cannes, France, MIPIM hosts twenty-six thousand participants from one hundred countries. Over the last few years, this real estate gathering has managed to weave PropTech into its more traditional education and events fabric. (See the resources section at the back of the book for a listing of PropTech events and more.)

In addition to attending a growing list of PropTech events, entrepreneurs, investors, and real estate practitioners try to stay in touch and up to date through news sources such as Bisnow.com, which covers commercial real estate generally but has pivoted in recent years to concentrate heavily on real estate technology, and PropModo (US) and PlaceTech (UK), which squarely focus on PropTech. MetaProp does its part here, too, as a go-to source for a wide range of media outlets. Our own information channels include the MetaProp blog (www.MetaProp.org/blog), our newsletter (www.MetaProp.org/newsletter), our podcast (www.MetaProp.org/the-metapropcast), and our Innovation Conversations series, the model for that feature in each chapter of this book. (Again, see resources section at the back of the book for important sources of news and information on PropTech.)

We founded the annual Global PropTech Awards and, each year, publish the PropTech Global Confidence Index based on our international survey in partnership with the Royal Institution of Chartered Surveyors and the Real Estate Board of New York. We have joined other companies, consultants, and academics in helping to produce a young but growing body of research about real estate technology and innovation. We have mentioned Zach's teaching at Columbia University, but we should note that he has created from scratch a unique and exciting space for PropTech within the masters of real estate development program at Columbia's Graduate School of Architecture, Planning, and Preservation.

Education is a key part of the PropTech community and most visible in our efforts with the MetaProp Accelerator at Columbia University. An *accelerator,* as the name implies, seeks to speed up and facilitate the development process for early-stage start-ups. A number of accelerators, including several devoted exclusively or largely to PropTech, have sprung up in recent years. Our own twenty-two-week program provides early-stage PropTech start-ups with up to $250,000 in financing, an advanced real estate curriculum, and pairing with top mentors from the industry. Entrepreneurs learn how to create a solid business plan. They learn how to make effective presentations and to create a succinct elevator pitch. They gain access to PropTech events and networking. Our extensive web of corporate partners not only gives invaluable feedback and advice but often provides early distribution for start-ups that aren't sure how to break into their market.

A large part of the community concept is about connecting entrepreneurs and start-ups with legacy companies, fostering partnerships, pilot programs, and product testing, as well as investment. We do this in all sorts of ways. One of the most important is by offering participants in our accelerator classes curated access to key industry decision makers, as well as to sources of capital, and media. Accelerators facilitate growth very effectively in a company's critical early days, which is why a number of the start-up founders whom we have quoted lament the fact that there were almost no accelerators around when they started out. Today, in addition to Y Combinator, the progenitor of all accelerators, MetaProp, 500 Startups, Techstars, Plug and Play, and others are nurturing start-ups and contributing to a burgeoning PropTech ecosystem.

The term ecosystem has become something of a cliché in business. However, it's tough to find a term that better conveys the many strands that connect early-stage PropTech start-ups to industry, the levels of interdependence in partnerships, investment, and community, and the incredible growth that occurs when the circles of our Venn diagram overlap in productive ways. In fact, MetaProp and our partners have an exciting pipeline of new, global

PropTech community innovations planned for 2019 and 2020. In the next chapter, we'll look at the other side of this coin, examining how industry can effectively engage with start-ups and PropTech to innovate and gain competitive advantage.

INNOVATION CONVERSATION

Nick Romito, founder and CEO, VTS

MetaProp: What were the greatest obstacles to success for VTS as a PropTech start-up?

Nick Romito: At the highest level, convincing lots of people who make lots of money that they have a problem. Change management is hard enough, but when people are very successful, they almost become naive to the issues. We had to spend a lot of time educating the market about how much more successful they could be if they had the same tools as people in other industries.

MetaProp: VTS and Hightower was a major, successful merger among PropTech start-ups. Do you see more mergers coming?

Nick Romito: I think you're going to continue to see consolidation happen in this space. The market is very large in terms of capital allocated and dollars available. It's a huge market, but you don't have a lot of customers. I think there are probably three thousand commercial landlords ... In a vertical market, most companies have to grow via acquisition to get to any reasonable size. CoStar, for example, has done a lot of deals. Look at the brokerage firms. I think CBRE does an acquisition a month. It's one of those places where I don't believe there can be 500 companies.

MetaProp: Do you see acquisitions of PropTech start-ups by traditional real estate companies increasing in the next few years?

Nick Romito: I do, and from the VTS perspective, it's 100 percent a part of our strategy. We're going to do more acquisitions. But if you look at some of the other real estate firms, they're getting their feet wet by starting these funds. They're either investing in funds like yours, or others, or they're creating their own, off the balance sheet, as Brookfield did ... The next logical phase is to start buying, potentially, if they think it's going to help their business.

MetaProp: Do you expect VTS to be acquired someday?

Nick Romito: I don't know if we would be acquired or go public. I don't think our investors would mind us doing an IPO in a couple of years, but lucky for us, we've got a very healthy business and plenty of time to figure that out.

MetaProp: How do you decide when it's the right time to raise further funding rounds, versus using your financial resources to go after more clients?

Nick Romito: I think that's another one where you got to look at your business and decide ... As a founder, you've got to be very honest with yourself and figure out, is this a just-add-water situation? Meaning, if I put $10 in, can I really get $20 or $30 out? If I can't do that, then I should not raise the money yet. I'm not ready. Just raising money to raise money is a horrible strategy, but people do it all the time. People always congratulate me for raising a round. That's like getting congratulated for taking out a mortgage on your house. It doesn't make a whole lot of sense. You're playing with someone else's money. Celebrate the ability to go and execute your vision, but don't celebrate someone giving you money. You didn't win. Someone gave you the opportunity to then go and win.

MetaProp: How do you see the future of PropTech start-ups? Is it getting easier or harder to start a company?

Nick Romito: I think, from a capital perspective, it's much easier. When we first launched and came out of stealth mode to announce the business in 2012, I don't know that there had been any venture capital at all spent in a commercial real estate ... But [the field] is a lot more competitive. It's not that you're competing necessarily from a product perspective; you're competing for mindshare. These are folks who are really busy, barely have time to do their own jobs and are getting twenty, thirty calls a day. As a technology company, you have to be able to tell your story and the value you provide very clearly and very quickly.

MetaProp: How do you interact with your investors? Are their expectations in line with yours about the growth of your company?

Nick Romito: Yes, we are totally aligned. They approve our annual budget. They approve of our overall strategy. It's what they signed up for. I think of them as an extension of the business, not as a body that I report to. When you're looking at taking capital from investors, you have to think about that. These are folks who you need to think are going to have your back, good or bad. Good quarter or bad quarter, they believe in the vision.

MetaProp: How do you see the future development and adoption by the industry of PropTech start-ups in the short run, say one to two years, and then in the longer run?

Nick Romito: I think the consolidation that we're going to see will be helpful. You probably have lots of great companies right now that are not being adopted simply because there's a lot of noise in the market. When those products or features become parts of companies like VTS or others that are largely adopted by the market, you're going to see people using more and more technologies. I think consolidation is actually going to help drive the adoption of technology in the space because too much decentralization or bifurcation is the original problem we set out to solve. I think it'll help the companies themselves, but it's also going to help push the market a little bit further, a little bit faster.

CHAPTER SIX

Industry Strategies for Engaging with PropTech

"A lot of real estate companies were led by people who didn't grow up with technology, and so it's unfamiliar and unknown, and we kind of dabble in it. Today, every company has to be a technology company, and you have to realize it's a tool to implement strategy. In other words, it has to be a core underlying principle, not just a thing on the side."

—**Lisa Picard**, president and CEO, EQ Office

"Patience and persistence work together. We have met with a number of start-ups who have come back to us over and over again as their product iterates and grows. The first time, or maybe two or three times, they came to us and it wasn't the right fit, but the fourth time around, it was."

—**Michael Rudin**, senior vice president, Rudin Management

Start-ups offer incumbents ways to boost revenue, address threats, find solutions, and reignite their entrepreneurial spirit. Legacy companies often enter the space defensively but learn to play offense and make money as they become tier one innovators in the synergistic zone where partnerships, investment, and community multiply opportunities.

Bowery, the tech-enabled appraisal business we mentioned in chapter 3, did not exactly sweep Cushman & Wakefield off its feet the first time the start-up encountered the commercial real estate giant.

"Two young guys came in and, as part of their pitch, showed all these old white guys sitting at their desks, looking tired, surrounded by piles of paper," Adam Stanley, Cushman's global CIO and chief digital officer, told us in an interview.

At the time, Bowery was in the MetaProp accelerator, turning an innovative concept into a scalable business, and Stanley had graciously offered to host a practice session for our annual Demo Day, when start-ups pitch their businesses to an international audience of investors, entrepreneurs, and corporate executives. Demo Day is a big deal, preceded by lots of practice, and lots of coaching. Stanley had assembled colleagues in both business and technology to hear start-up presentations and provide feedback. Unfortunately, the image of frustrated old white guys awash in paper wasn't winning anyone over.

"They basically painted the picture that that was our appraisal business," Stanley laughs. "In the room were a few of those older white guys, and, of course, they start to just attack, like, 'Yeah, we've automated a lot more than that' and 'There are all these regulations you're not taking into account,'" and so on.

Bowery's platform integrates public records and an extensive comp database to digitize and automate the flow of information that appraisers usually gather through painstaking processes. Its technology creates reports that are more consistent and accurate, as well as faster, than the industry average. The platform was impressive even in those early days, but a vocal contingent of the industry audience insisted that Bowery's technology wouldn't work for them. Stanley understood that feathers had been ruffled and framed the question in practical terms.

"After Bowery left, I said to my team, the technology part of the room, 'Look, we have three options as I see it: we can ignore them, kill them, or join them,'" Stanley told us. "'And I need you guys to tell me which one it should be.'"

Stanley was perfectly willing to ignore the start-up if his tech team could convince him that Cushman's appraisal service was better than Bowery's and always would be, that this start-up would never pose a threat. "Killing" Bowery required coming up with technology that would make Bowery irrelevant. Could his team produce that? The third option, initially discounted out of hand, was to join the start-up as a partner.

"About a month later, the team came back after several meetings with Bowery and, basically, said, 'We think we should join them,'" Stanley told us. "The business leaders who had been complete naysayers said they were impressed, and we formed a partnership."

Why Engage with PropTech?

It's easy to say, in 2018, that the real estate industry must engage with technology. It's almost a platitude, but explaining exactly why and how is complicated, as the Cushman-Bowery narrative illustrates. We like this story as much as Adam Stanley does partly because it displays so many of the dynamics, pitfalls, and benefits intrinsic to corporate partnerships with start-ups.

In this case, a legacy company faces a tech-based start-up that is a potential competitor for appraisal business. Is it a threat, an opportunity, or neither? This is, essentially, what Stanley asked his team to decide with the three options he presented: ignore, kill, or join.

Once the Cushman team determined that Bowery's technology had potential, ignoring it would have been risky. The start-up would not have ignored its rivals, including Cushman, and if the enterprise company had not partnered with Bowery, one of Cushman's big competitors might have. Eliminating Bowery as a threat by coming up with better technology would have been expensive, time-consuming, and far removed from Cushman's core business, if it were even possible.

Instead, the two companies made a deal that would be exclusive while Cushman helped the start-up refine its product but would then allow Bowery to license its technology elsewhere. Later, we'll explore the complex technological, financial, and cultural dimensions of such partnerships, but first, we want to briefly highlight just a few of the reasons why they make sense for industry.

ADDRESS THREATS

We began this book with a discussion of the dramatic changes PropTech is precipitating in real estate and the attendant threats for firms that are slow to adapt. If additional revenue is not incentive enough to engage with technology, how about survival?

This is no exaggeration. In 2017, as we mentioned in chapter 1, SoftBank invested $4.4 billion in coworking company WeWork and its subsidiaries. This tech-enabled firm and others, such as Knotel, Industrious, Convene, and TechSpace, are changing the way office space is not just leased, managed, and configured but conceptualized too. To remain competitive, commercial real estate firms will need to offer space that has more energy and services, according to Lisa Picard, and they'll need to do so in less time, with more flexible terms. Technology is the backbone of such efforts.

As EQ started its $500 million addition to the base of Chicago's Willis Tower (formerly, Sears Tower), it signed up Convene for a large chunk of the new square footage. The PropTech company's branded conference and event space will attract tenants and help EQ modernize its offerings, making it more competitive with the likes of WeWork. In a couple of New York projects, Rudin Management is avoiding the threat of WeWork not by offering similar amenities but by offering the *same* ones. Dock 72, Rudin's second collaboration with the coworking start-up, will include a half-court basketball facility, a ten thousand-square-foot lawn, a health and wellness center, a food and beverage facility, a conference and event space, and the trademark events and social networking that WeWork is known for.

Real estate technology can help companies address the threat of functional obsolescence everywhere from an individual outdated building to a changing business model. On the residential front, Zillow and others are moving closer to the transaction, reducing consumers' reliance on agents. Compass, meanwhile, has raised nearly $800 million and is taking new markets by storm, snapping up top agents with promises of higher commissions and cutting-edge technology.

Smart brokerages that can't afford to ignore these hungry new competitors or to develop rival technologies of their own are turning to PropTech start-ups to counter the threat, with solutions for everything from online marketing to lead cultivation. Fees and margins are threatened, not just for residential agents but also for commercial brokers, mortgage brokers, title companies, and others. By offering new ways to improve service and add revenue, PropTech can help companies stay ahead of fee compression.

Earlier, we documented the threat that Amazon and other online retailers pose to physical stores. Start-ups such as LocateAI, which uses machine learning to forecast the revenue of potential store sites, analyze market potential, and more, can help brick-and-mortar retailers survive and prosper. Many physical retailers underestimated Amazon, just as commercial landlords underestimated WeWork, which is morphing from simple coworking in rapid and not always predictable ways. Competitive threats no longer come only from companies that look like one another. A new crop of highly capitalized, technologically sophisticated players can move into new terrain and pose new threats overnight.

We could fill another book with such examples, but we hope we have made the point that while PropTech can be a threat to incumbents, for the open-minded, it also becomes a way to counter threats. Strategically, we think of engagement with PropTech as both defense and offense for real estate firms, as we'll explore shortly. Addressing threats, the defensive end of the continuum, is a common starting point for firms on their way to becoming what we call tier one innovators.

FIND SOLUTIONS

One of our favorite PropTech stories, and one of the earliest of the internet age, is the tale of 55 Broad Street, a tower that emptied precipitously in the early '90s when Rudin Management's tenant Drexel Burnham Lambert closed, literally overnight. Rudin, a venerable family-run business started in the '20s, suddenly had an empty office tower at a time when lower Manhattan alone had tens of millions of square feet of vacant space.

"That's obviously not a position you want to find yourself in overnight," Michael Rudin, who, at the time, was a kid but who is now a senior vice president at the company, told us. "But what that did afford us was the ability to take a step back and say, 'How can we differentiate ourselves?'"

Rudin's father and the company's new COO read *Being Digital,* Nicholas Negroponte's visionary book about the transition to a digital future, and decided that technology might provide a solution. The internet was in its infancy then, but Negroponte highlighted the economic role it could, eventually, play and sketched an office building of the future: a fully wired tower focused on connectivity and data services.

Rudin installed the latest technology in 55 Broad Street, with carrier-neutral risers, a dedicated rooftop satellite farm, and one of the first websites ever for a commercial building, rebranded as the New York Information Technology Center. Within eighteen months of reopening, the roughly four hundred thousand-square-foot office tower was fully leased, largely to telecom and media companies, and Rudin started applying the same approach in its other buildings.

The Rudins were on the cutting edge. Twenty years later, legacy companies are finally beginning to appreciate the wide range of solutions that technology can provide across the real estate value chain, especially through partnerships with and investments in early-stage PropTech start-ups.

Commercial real estate firm CBRE, for example, wanted a better way for clients to visualize space and take virtual tours. It found a solution by buying Floored, a start-up whose interactive 2-D and 3-D graphics allow for virtual customization, space layout, and walk-throughs. Blackstone's strategic investment in VTS gave it a premier system for tracking real-time leasing data and portfolio performance, and its investment in Entic's smart building technology brought quick energy savings at a number of assets. Brookfield has found solutions by partnering with and investing in a number of start-ups we have mentioned, including BuildingConnected and Convene, among others.

Hotels, retailers of all sizes, small landlords, and even Airbnb hosts also are finding solutions, streamlining operations, and serving their customers better with PropTech. As we'll see later in this chapter, leveraging start-ups for tech solutions allows industry players of all sizes to test many products and services cheaply to find the optimal ones, and, often, to influence their development.

Engaging with PropTech is a way for companies to participate in the macroeconomic changes underway as early adopters or fast followers, instead of becoming dinosaurs.

Engaging with PropTech is a way for companies to participate in the macroeconomic changes underway as early adopters or fast followers, instead of becoming dinosaurs.

GROW REVENUE

When this book went to press, Cushman had made more than $1 million as a result of its partnership with Bowery.

"This was all new business for us because it was in a space that we weren't actually doing a lot of work in, prior," Stanley told us.

In chapter 3 we documented various ways in which PropTech is producing revenue for industry players, so we won't belabor the point here. Suffice it to say that every start-up mentioned in the last chapter is improving processes and/or making money for its corporate partners. Companies that ignore emerging tech solutions are leaving money on the table.

Typically, firms that enter the space for defensive reasons begin to see opportunities, the ways that PropTech can provide new revenue streams and business lines, over time. This is a key part of becoming a tier one innovator, a process we'll discuss later.

CHANGE CULTURE

Perhaps the most important reason for industry to partner with early-stage PropTech start-ups is also the least appreciated. Jim Stengel sums up the idea nicely in his book *Unleashing the Innovators,* where he recalls his realization, as global marketing officer for Procter & Gamble, that the massive old company needed new life:[76]

> Why did we need start-ups? Not just because they offered indispensable products and services to P&G, but because they did business in a radically different way. They were engines of continual creativity; they engaged passionately with their audiences and customers; they hired the best and the brightest people, people who loved working there. In fact, they were sparking a dangerous talent drain away from mature companies like ours.

---

76 Jim Stengel, *Unleashing the Innovators: How Mature Companies Find New Life with Startups,* (New York: Crown Business, 2017).

PropTech engagement spurs innovation within organizations. It isn't simply about buying or adopting tech solutions from outside. It allows in-house talent to evolve. This culture shift also gives companies access to tomorrow's leaders as a large group of older executives begins to retire, the "silver tsunami" so often written about.

According to Adam Stanley, Cushman & Wakefield has prioritized partnerships with start-ups as Bowery has, for cultural reasons, but he acknowledges that changing culture at a large established company is not without pain:

> We were able to kind of practice [with Bowery]. I think we learned some things that we would probably want to change in the future. One of the things we've learned is that it's hard working with start-ups, sometimes. You know, I think Bowery has something like nineteen or twenty employees, and we have 48,000. We have more lawyers working for our company than they have employees.

Stanley's view reflects a sea change in how the real estate industry sees PropTech. Earlier, we quoted the KPMG report "Bridging the Gap: How the Real Estate Sector Can Engage with PropTech to Bring the Built and Digital Environments Together." Around 90 percent of survey respondents in that report thought technological change would impact their business and agreed that traditional real estate organizations need to engage with PropTech companies to adapt to the changing global environment. Only 34 percent, however, had an enterprise-wide digital strategy.[77]

This state of affairs goes a long way toward explaining the results of another survey done by venture capital fund and accelerator 500 Startups. The report of this survey, "Unlocking Innovation through

---

77   KPMG, op. cit.

Startup Engagement," found that most corporations see fewer than 25 percent of their initial pilots with start-ups scale into solutions that can be taken to market.[78]

Collaborating with start-ups is complicated for enterprise companies, even the ones dedicated to making such partnerships work. We have seen the equation from both sides. Before founding MetaProp, both of us had experience with both tech start-ups and legacy real estate companies. We have built MetaProp's advisory activities around that experience and the best practices that, we have learned, allow these relationships to flourish.

Companies that don't have clear strategies for engaging with PropTech are likely to waste enormous amounts of time, energy, and money. In the remainder of this chapter, we'll share some of the lessons we've learned from acting as a bridge between industry and PropTech.

Build It, Buy It, or Partner

Industry has three basic options when it comes to technology: (1) build your own, (2) buy a ready-made product, or (3) form partnerships to test and help create it. The KPMG report, "Bridging the Gap," concludes that "grow-your-own is rarely an option when it comes to PropTech. Partnerships will be key." Only 17 percent of

Industry has three basic options when it comes to technology: (1) build your own, (2) buy a ready-made product, or (3) form partnerships to test and help create it.

---

78 "Unlocking Innovation through Startup Engagement," 500 Startups, June 2017, https://www.slideshare.net/amalistclient/unlocking-innovation-in-global-corporations-june-2017.

respondents to KPMG's survey said they planned to develop their own tech innovations.[79]

The reasons for not pursuing tech in-house will be obvious to most readers. Developing your own tech solution is expensive and time consuming. For a real estate company, it's far afield of the core business and competencies. It offers more control but is limiting in other ways. Rather than testing multiple solutions, it forces a company to commit to one, which might nor might not do the job.

A rare exception to the trend away from in-house tech development is Rudin Management's creation of Nantum. This is a building operating system originally designed for owners and managers and later expanded to serve tenants, and later still, individual employees. Michael Rudin told us that his company first tried to buy a system off the shelf but, back in the 2000s, couldn't find anything suitable. The Rudins formed their own PropTech company, Prescriptive Data, and began developing Nantum in 2010. The first iteration launched in 2013. Today, it runs across Rudin Management's commercial portfolio, as well as in outside properties. Dock 72 will be the first building to test the individual employee app.

"You get the most bang for your buck and the most data and intel and operational efficiencies if you have all three running [building, tenant, and employee systems] but they can all function as stand-alone or in any combination," Rudin told us. Nantum, which uses machine learning and artificial intelligence, is also compatible with other systems and data feeds. "We're not smart enough to create the solution for every problem that we have, but we want to be able to integrate and allow various solutions to talk to each other."

The system is saving Rudin Management around fifty cents per square foot annually—$5 million a year across its ten-million-square-

79   KPMG, op. cit.

foot portfolio, according to Rudin, including a 24 percent reduction in total electric consumption and a 47 percent reduction in steam consumption. The experience of rolling out Nantum also highlighted for Michael Rudin and others at the company that its portfolio provided a great sandbox for testing new technologies. Gradually, Rudin Management began piloting solutions, investing in and partnering with select start-ups relevant to the core business, including Enertiv (an IoT system complementary to Nantum) and Radiator Labs, whose Cozy made sense for Rudin's steam-heated residential properties.

Rudin designed its own building operating system with Nantum only reluctantly, after it couldn't find a good turn-key solution. There are many solid off-the-shelf tech options, and most companies use a variety of them, but the dilemma Rudin Management faced is a common one.

Vendors, typically, provide yesterday's technology. Late-stage PropTech companies, as we've said, provide today's technology as it's waiting to scale. Early-stage PropTech is vital to innovation because it truly is tomorrow's technology waiting to be proven. This is where the most creative, cutting-edge solutions are found. Early-stage PropTech offers the most advanced tech. It offers industry partners who get in on the ground floor a serious competitive advantage and the chance to provide feedback and shape a product's development without the risk associated with building their own solutions. Legacy companies gain speed, access to a wide range of expertise they don't always have, and a chance to see problems through fresh eyes.

Playing Offense and Defense with PropTech

We hope we have made the case for *why* industry must engage with PropTech. The *how* becomes much more complex. Innovation is occurring at a dizzying pace. There is an onslaught of new start-ups, constant news of mergers and acquisitions, and announcements of significant investments. Partnerships can be complicated and difficult to navigate. Open innovation looks a lot like chaos because, well, it is. Making sense of that chaos, however, is our full-time job at MetaProp. One of the tools we use to help real estate companies understand the space is our PropTech Engagement Funnel, pictured below.

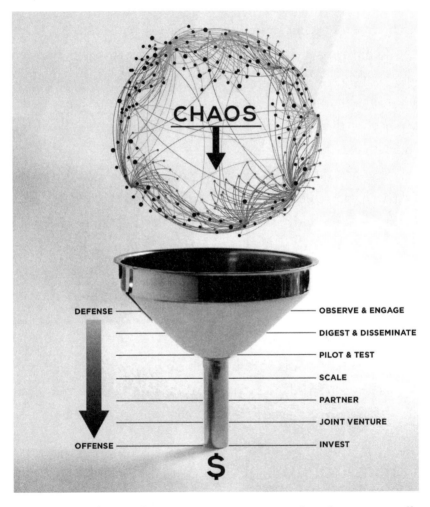

The swirling sphere on top represents the chaotic, rapidly changing world of PropTech start-ups. Many incumbents enter the space defensively as they note a revenue stream under threat, a competitor with a tech advantage, a changing business model, and so on. Over time, they develop offensive strategies, too, using real estate technology to gain competitive advantage, create new revenue, offering new services, and so on. PropTech no longer appears as simply a threat but becomes both threat and opportunity. As are the best sports teams, the firms that we often refer to as tier 1 innovators are adept at both offense and defense.

In our experience working with large owners, developers, managers, construction, and brokerage firms, we have noted that the successful journey to becoming a tier-1 innovator tends to happen in the three stages designated in our PropTech Engagement Funnel. The Funnel is a synthesis and visual representation of many of the ideas we have been discussing and rests on three core competencies that we will explore in the last section of this chapter.

STAGE ONE

Observe and engage. Firms need a way to see the broadest set of potential disruptors to their existing business and to important and sometimes unexpected adjacent businesses. They also need an efficient channel for two-way communications with innovators about individual and firm strategies, interests, and capabilities.

Digest and disseminate. Firms need to understand, track, and make sense of their observations. The knowledge they're gaining must be regularly disseminated to the right people throughout the organization.

STAGE TWO

Pilot and test. Often known as proof of concept (POC), piloting requires a mechanism for evaluating qualified opportunities and quickly engaging in small test programs that are likely to fail. (Many fast failures are the quickest route to success.) Sophisticated organizations approaching tier one status test in a designated sandbox, or proving ground, which can be organized by real estate asset (or portion of an asset), by operating unit, by team, and so on. Pilots also can also be deployed opportunistically into a business, tested when and where the fit feels right. Such test drives are a chance to learn, build relationships, and, hopefully, enjoy an early win or two. Sometimes real estate organizations can even help to mold the product to address specific business needs.

Scale. Once a pilot or test is deemed successful, larger organizations frequently require broad application and distribution of the technology in order to achieve needle-moving impact. A lot can go wrong here. Large companies can smother small ones, start-ups can run out of money, start-up staffing might be inadequate for quick growth, and so on.

STAGE 3

Partner, or joint venture. If a technology has the potential to scale, a real estate company must be able to connect commercially and strategically with the start-up. Such collaborations can look like traditional vendor relationships or true partnerships in which the parties explore new business lines together. Partnering often overlaps with scaling. (None of these steps are strictly linear.)

Invest. Strategic investing is a powerful tool but, as with other steps in the funnel, it's fraught with risk. Financial gain is, obviously, one important reason to invest, but other reasons are often more important including the ability to support growth, influence a team, gain exclusivity, and establish a path to merger/acquisition. Investments and the appearance of influencing investments—for example, via fund or other direct investment vehicles—is a critical competency, as we will see in the Venn diagram of core competencies that we explore below.

Bringing PropTech into the Real Estate Tent

At MetaProp, we spend an enormous amount of time and energy to help firms at various stages in the funnel engage with PropTech and to facilitate corporate-start-up relationships on the road to becoming tier-one innovators. As we noted in describing the ultimately successful partnership of Bowery and Cushman & Wakefield, the terrain between a small, nimble start-up trying to shake up industry and a massive corporation embedded in it—with diverse stakeholders and established processes—is tricky. The three core competencies for successful corporate engagement with PropTech, we have found, are the same as those that allow start-ups to successfully engage with industry: (1) partnerships, (2) investments, and (3) community.

Just as many firms begin by playing defense before developing offensive PropTech strategies, companies also tend to start in just one of the circles in the diagram above, depending on firm culture. An entrepreneurial investment firm usually starts on the venture, or investment, side. A conservative firm often begins on the partnership side. A firm with current brand-centric needs, such as Zillow or PwC, might start on the community side. In our experience, though, in order to become a tier 1 innovator, every firm gradually moves to the "middle," taking part in investment, partnerships, and community.

We are devoting chapter 7 entirely to investment, so we won't spend much time on it here. For now, we'll just say that enterprises we've mentioned, including Blackstone, Cushman & Wakefield, EQ Office, and CBRE invest in PropTech start-ups with good reason. Early-stage investments, which pay for solutions the companies hope to use later, help to produce or refine products, often in conjunction with pilots. They also up the level of commitment and trust on both sides. Industrial investments give some measure of control, sometimes even customization, and down the road, can bring solid returns (not that this is, typically, the primary motivation).

We'll return to investment in the next chapter in order to focus here on partnerships and community.

Building Partnerships

DO AN INNOVATION ASSESSMENT

As with any relationship, self-awareness contributes to a healthy corporate start-up partnership. (Our apologies in advance if this section sounds a little like couples counseling, but many of the same principles apply.) We recommend starting with an innovation assessment. What do you need? What do you want? What capabilities and strengths do you bring to the table? Where are the pain points crying out for tech-based innovation in your organization? Where are the weak spots in your tech staffing? A shocking number of companies, including some sizeable ones, still rely on a single CIO, or "the IT guy," to handle technology. If this book does nothing else, we hope it drives home the point that, in today's fast-moving tech environment, the IT guy no longer cuts it.

MetaProp's advising activities offer partners innovation assessments, often as part of our consulting on digital transformation, and we know from experience that these assessments can be daunting. They do not, however, need to be completed overnight. In fact, a process should be established to continually assess and reassess tech readiness. This is not a one-time exercise, and the initial aim is not complete transformation but identification of and prioritization of important goals and problems. For example, MetaProp's industry advisory teams regularly run two- to four-hour ideation and innovation workshops with groups of six to twenty-five client business heads, division leaders, and emerging professionals.

As MetaProp partner Philip Russo put it when we interviewed him:

> The hardest part for an incumbent real estate firm is to not grab at every shiny PropTech start-up that crosses its path. Aligning internal business goals and objectives, short-term and long, while maintaining self-discipline in applying them to the start-ups assessed and piloted is vital to success. However, that's just the front end of the process. The much harder back end is to then get the company's business leaders to buy in and champion what the technology and outside advisors have brought to the table after a thorough vetting process. That's usually the weakest link in the chain of transformation from a company that uses tech to one that is actually a real estate technology firm.

As Ernst and Young (EY) points out in its report, "How Are Engineering and Construction Companies Adapting Digital to Their Businesses?" the first round of assessment can often be done with minimal investment: "With a well-planned strategy and an honest assessment of your digital readiness, the areas of critical importance should become apparent. Often, in the beginning stages, the resources needed are nominal, and assessment of critical flaws along value chain activities can be identified using a small team."[80]

Beginning with gaps and real problems within the organization avoids what Adam Stanley called in our interview the hammer-in-search-of-a-nail approach. PropTech is about real innovation for real problems and real growth, not superfluous gadgets and apps.

"Until you define the problems and have a strategy around what you're trying to solve, it's going to be really tough," Ryan Simonetti of Convene told us. "You're just going to get inundated with solutions, and what you don't want to do is chase shiny toys around, right? Because that doesn't drive business outcomes."

BUILD A TEAM

Every real estate company, no matter how small, needs someone in charge of technology. We are not arguing that tech should be segregated or become *only* one person's job. In fact, it must become a part of everyone's job, but someone needs to be the gatekeeper for PropTech, assessing the company's internal tech needs and filtering the many possible solutions. Someone needs to be the point person whom start-ups can approach. As Lisa Picard said in our interview:

One of the first things I did when I came onboard was to hire a vice president of real estate tech. As you can imagine, being the CEO of a real estate company owned by Blackstone, we get a lot of requests and a lot of pings.

---

80   Ernst and Young, "How Are Engineering and Construction Companies Adapting Digital to Their Businesses?" accessed December 2, 2018, https://www.ey.com/Publication/vwLUAssets/EY-Digital-survey/$File/EY-Digital-survey.pdf.

It's a lot easier for me to say, "Hey, go talk to Ryan. He's our head of real estate tech. He evaluates all the PropTech, its value to our overall organizational strategy, and then says what we should pursue."

Those overseeing tech solutions should have adequate resources: a budget and team that allow them to manage change and stoke innovation. Equally important, as Picard emphasized, the tech chief—whether that person's title is vice president of real estate technology, chief information officer, chief technology officer, or something else—must be a part of top leadership. That person must have real power to make change, "which is why," Picard told us, "our head of real estate tech is part of our executive leadership team."

The competition for talented technologists is fierce these days, which can make assembling a tech team challenging. In the same EY survey quoted previously, a lack of trained staff to review, implement, and operate digital technologies was number two among the challenges to digital transformation.[81]

We regularly see this issue firsthand in MetaProp's advisory activities, where we also help legacy companies with real estate tech recruitment and employee training. In fact, we've sourced, placed, and/or deeply engaged with a half dozen first-time PropTech leaders over the past two years. Partnering with early-stage start-ups, of course, is a way to leverage tech expertise, and the rise of PropTech in recent years is gradually improving the real estate industry's image among job seekers. Incumbents who show a commitment to innovation and embrace technology obviously have an easier time recruiting young talent.

---

81   Ernst and Young, op. cit.

ESTABLISH A PROCESS

Start-ups have much to learn from legacy companies, and they know it. Many mature companies, however, fail in their partnerships with start-ups because they don't understand that learning in this relationship is a two-way street. While start-ups are acclimating to corporate culture, procurement, and decision making, smart incumbents use these collaborations to jump-start what Jim Stengel in *Unleashing the Innovators* calls their "entrepreneurial DNA."[82]

PropTech start-ups can put incumbents back in touch with their own early-stage energy, making them nimbler, more creative, faster, and leaner if corporate leaders meet them halfway. Having a solid process in place for dealing with start-ups and implementing tests is vital not just for improving pilots' success rates, but also for rekindling the spirit of innovation and building an openness to new ideas, strategies, and technologies.

The process can and should vary from organization to organization, matching the personality and resources of each company. Since we started this chapter with an example of a Cushman & Wakefield partnership, we will briefly review that company's process. We know it well because we have advised Cushman on PropTech, but we also happen to think it's an excellent model. So does *CIO Magazine*, which gave Cushman a CIO 100 Award in 2018 for the process it calls "proof of concept as a service" (POCaaS).

The philosophy behind the process is simple, according to Stanley: make start-ups feel welcome. "We decided four years ago that we wanted to make ourselves the company that start-ups would want to work with," he told us. "We basically said, 'What can we do to create a culture where they know they're welcome?'"

---

82   Jim Stengel with Tom Post, *Unleashing the Innovators: How Mature Companies Find New Life with Startups,* (New York, New York: Crown Business 2017).

As we noted above, that culture begins with self-awareness. In a database, Stanley tracks Cushman's needs: requests from Cushman executives around the world for tech-based solutions that the company has not yet been able to deliver. If a start-up seems relevant, Stanley will gauge interest among those lodging related requests. If the start-up doesn't appear to meet a current need, a team member does a one-page write-up about it and parks this summary in a kind of catalog, where it's categorized by various tags: blockchain, AI, lease transaction, and so on. As new needs surface, the tech team can quickly reference its list of start-ups: *Oh yeah, companies X and Y are both working on that problem.*

AIM FOR SPEED AND EASE

The master services agreements (MSA) that Cushman signed with start-ups used to hover around thirty pages, which is not unusual in the corporate world, but which is burdensome for the start-up with $80,000 and an idea. Stanley whittled the standard agreement, which he thinks of as a prenup, down to a four-page document Cushman calls MSA lite.

"You have to learn a different way of interacting with a company that might be operating out of a garage versus HP or Microsoft," Stanley told us.

The tech team has an expedited process for meeting with start-ups to grasp what they do. If there is mutual interest, Stanley finds an executive sponsor no more than two levels below a division chief. This demonstrates a high degree of commitment to the start-up, which has to show that it can meet a need for a particular market or service line. If the executive thinks the solution has potential, a "business lead"—someone below the executive but still senior—runs a pilot program to test the product. The business lead establishes the hypothesis, sets success criteria, rallies the troops, and ultimately, recommends whether or not to move forward. The technology side of the pilot mirrors the business side, with one executive sponsor (always one of Stanley's direct reports) and one person below that sponsor leading the charge.

"We want to be nimble and we want to do it really quickly and we don't want to have a lot of bureaucracy," Stanley told us. "It's been really effective. We used to take off lots of planes and not land very many of them. Now we take off planes; we land them. We quickly decide whether or not we're going to try it again or just tell them thanks for playing, but no interest."

PATIENCE, FEEDBACK, RESULTS

A pilot is just that, and although we're emphasizing speed and agility, corporate partners must have patience too. They all want results, but results take time, thoughtful feedback from enterprises, and often, many iterations of the product. The committed corporate partner with a high level of engagement is often rewarded, as EQ Office has learned from working with a variety of early-stage PropTech start-ups.

"We particularly like when we can get in early, on the ground floor, and start to better the product," Picard said during our interview. "We can give them real-time feedback in terms of the dashboard, the information, and what on their roadmap makes the most sense for rapid deployment with us, or their attraction for other users."

EQ's feedback enabled VTS to retool its leasing approval process in a way that helped leadership understand the deal flow, for example, and helped perfect the data going into the application. EQ also is working with project management platform Honest Buildings on a capital planning tool that will give it real-time pricing on various capital projects, allowing the commercial giant to make comparisons across its portfolio.

The fail-fast, iterate-often model, in which many versions of a product can be quickly tested and tweaked, saves time and money in the long run. Corporate partners have the benefit of running pilots with lots of start-ups in order to cherry-pick the optimal solutions. According to Stanley:

> If you create a culture that, basically, says, "We want to be better at identifying quickly things we cannot do for our clients that they want us to do, and we have a way to send those demands out into the universe of accelerators, venture capital firms, and other start-up relationships, and receive back three, four, or five possible solutions," then we can be a much more successful company.

The concrete steps we've outlined above are all simply manifestations of a particular corporate mindset, a culture that values innovation and is open to new ideas, processes, technologies, and partners. PropTech, as we've said repeatedly, is not about technology so much as innovation. Its heart is not hardware or software but a cultural shift toward innovation.

According to Picard, "Every company has to be a technology company, and you have to realize it's a tool to implement strategy. In other words, it has to be a core underlying principle, not just a thing on the side."

Building Community

During the last two years, Cushman has looked at more than two hundred and fifty PropTech start-ups, according to Stanley, either directly or through partners such as MetaProp. His database lists around one hundred start-ups with a status of either active or on hold. The fifty or sixty that are on hold aren't relevant now, but he thinks they might be someday. Around ten have advanced to the pilot or partnership phase, and the rest are in the exploration phase.

Even with Cushman's rigorous system, tracking the enormous number of PropTech start-ups and potential solutions in the space is daunting, especially when it comes to the critical early stage, which offers the greatest return, the most opportunity for corporate input, and the biggest risk. Stanley has a group of about half a dozen people who are constantly in touch with universities, accelerators, and advisors who track the freshest start-ups. These team members attend PropTech events, contests, and conferences. They participate in practice sessions for the MetaProp Demo Day, which provides another link to the community and can cultivate partnerships such as the one with Bowery that resulted in new business.

As we have said elsewhere, if we had to boil down everything we do at MetaProp into one word, it would be *community* because it is so critical for both start-ups and industry. Community is how PropTech start-ups looking for industry connections, pilots, investment, and distribution succeed, and it's also how corporations, hungry for innovation, competitive advantage, better services, and new business, thrive.

Our deep connections to early-stage start-ups and industry,

> *Community is how PropTech start-ups looking for industry connections, pilots, investment, and distribution succeed, and it's also how corporations, hungry for innovation, competitive advantage, better services, and new business, thrive.*

our mentoring, advising, accelerating, event sponsoring, researching, and other activities are all designed to provide industry and start-ups with the richest possible network and maximize the number of contact points for executives, entrepreneurs, technologists, investors, media, enthusiasts, and others.

Investing is a vital part of community, the fuel powering the current PropTech wave. It is also an important part of our mission at MetaProp, important enough that we'll spend the entire next chapter exploring it.

INNOVATION CONVERSATION

Karen Hollinger, vice president of corporate initiatives, AvalonBay Communities

MetaProp: What is AvalonBay doing to engage with technology? What start-ups are being used?

Karen Hollinger: Well, it's probably a little early to name specific start-ups that we are piloting, but we are testing somewhere around fifty or sixty PropTech real start-ups around our portfolio. We are actively seeking new technologies and new companies that can add differentiation to the real estate portfolio, given its size and breadth.

MetaProp: Truly an amazing amount. What's spurring the usage?

Karen Hollinger: I would say the drive for innovation is increasing on both the consumer and corporate sides. Primarily, as our portfolio grows and the demographic to which we are catering expands, we realize that just being in the right location does not provide a differentiator for a specific demographic or a specific geography. Therefore, we need to look for technologies that provide either a customer-service benefit, an additional revenue stream, or lowered expense to each community. We will, in a risk-averse manner, try these out accordingly. Because we own our entire portfolio and manage this portfolio we're in an enviable position in that we don't have to approach a multitude of JB partners and investors in order to make quick decisions … Five to six years ago, as the investment in venture capital funds precipitated an increase in nontraditional technology players, they were approaching us on an asset-by-asset basis. We recognized that this does not provide economies of scale in vetting, increases our risk, and doesn't allow for a holistic view of the marketplace. Therefore, AvalonBay created the corporate initiative group, which has several functions, including being the primary assessment vehicle for all new technologies for our very broad portfolio.

MetaProp: As VP of corporate initiatives, how do you interact with PropTech?

Karen Hollinger: Well, I have an unusual position in PropTech because I have the need for the product or service. I have an R&D fund that's not tied to a specific asset budget, but we, typically, do not directly invest in funds where the fund manager is deciding on our behalf. I focus on ten to twelve VC *Shark Tank*-type conferences a year to get a broad view and establish relationships with the top twenty or twenty-five VCs in real estate PropTech and offer free advisory services for when they are considering an investment in an applicable company.

MetaProp: Where do you see PropTech continuing to add to AvalonBay's capabilities?

Karen Hollinger: Well, there are lots of companies that we are interested in and are piloting, but there have yet to be many real estate tech companies that have developed a service or product that is game changing to our industry. They're mostly auxiliary. They often don't work for seven-tenths of the portfolio for either the cost structure or the demo-graphic or the geography. There are a handful that could, if they evolve, actually change the way we develop, wholesale. I look forward to seeing that.

MetaProp: What do you see as the future of PropTech? Is the industry moving fast enough to assess and adopt various technologies?

Karen Hollinger: No. I would say the industry is not moving fast enough to assess and adopt. There are several reasons. There are very few big players, particularly in multifamily. I can think of maybe six. Of those six big players, I'd say three of them have a department or funds similar to AvalonBay, focused on that assessment, which means it is still episodic and will not actually return quick decision making. Further, our industry is, generally, very conservative because if you are a long-term holder, which many of the big players are, any decision that impacts the physical asset needs to last thirty years. If you add something that is physically impactful and make a decision, then you will be stripping it out of the asset in the next three to five years, and the cost will be wasted.

MetaProp: That's very well said. Is there anything else you'd like to add?

Karen Hollinger: More founders or organizational structures in these newcos need to have an actual understanding of real estate. I too often find that a newco at the series-A or, maybe, even series-B level will come in with a technology manifest and not actually understand how real estate works or how multifamily works. Their thesis is that multifamily must work the same as commercial or must work the same as single family. That is wholesale inaccurate. Yet our industry desires innovation and technology investment so wholeheartedly that we would give these newcos the benefit of our time early on to help them craft a business to fit our needs.

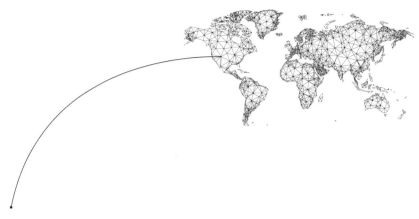

C H A P T E R   S E V E N

Investment and PropTech

"People fell in love with technology and it can become a 'tech thing.' I have this nice widget that allows you to do A, B, C, and then you say, 'That's great but where's the business? Where's the revenue? Where's the profit model?' It may take a while to get there if you are a venture early-stage company, and you may pivot from one model to another model, but tell me the model."

—**Nadeem Shaikh,** founder and former CEO, Anthemis Group

"There are moments when there is an opportunity to create a large, enduring company and moments when the industry or consumer is not ready to adopt a change. It is important to recognize those moments because if you are five years early on the idea, it is the same as being wrong."

—**Stuart Ellman,** cofounder and general partner, RRE Ventures

---

After years of being ignored by investors, PropTech has seen a flood of new venture capital. Tracking this chaotic, exciting space and analyzing potential investments is extremely difficult. MetaProp's early-stage investment strategy focuses on agility, healthy follow-on investments, market and product potential, and, most of all, people.

When Pete Flint was looking for investors to fund Trulia back in 2005, he met with a top venture capitalist. The investor said he understood the problem that the start-up was trying to solve and that he was excited about the team, but, unfortunately, no one made money investing in online real estate. There were structural reasons, he said, that made this an unappealing area for investment.

"Literally, no one had built a successful online real estate company at that time," Flint said in our interview. "There was a perception within venture communities that it was almost an uninvestible category."

Less than ten years later, after a successful IPO, Trulia was acquired by Zillow for $3.5 billion. That company had also seen runaway growth, enough to pay that hefty price for its competitor. Surely, by 2012, the year Michael Mandel cofounded CompStak—the crowdsourcing platform for sharing commercial comp data—investors had warmed to real estate technology?

Not much, according to Mandel, whom we also interviewed.

"There was no such thing as the CRE tech space or real estate tech space," Mandel told us. "There was zero interest from the VC community in real estate tech. It was a complete uphill battle to get anyone to even take this space seriously."

Fast-forward to 2018. At MetaProp, we closed our second venture capital fund, a $40 million vehicle called MetaProp Ventures II, with limited partners including RXR Realty, PGIM Real Estate, Cushman & Wakefield, CBRE, JLL Spark, and other blue-chip firms. The previous year, PropTech VC giant Fifth Wall Ventures made waves when it announced that it had raised $212 million, mostly from enterprise real estate companies such as CBRE, Equity Residential, and Lennar Corp., for its first fund.

Los Angeles-based Navitas Capital has emerged as a prominent VC fund focused on real estate technology, while Chicago-based Moderne Ventures aims for broader tech start-ups, but with real estate applications.

In addition to investing in venture capital funds focused on real estate, a number of legacy companies have started their own venture arms. JLL created JLL Spark, a new division led by Silicon Valley entrepreneurs, to invest in real estate technology, and Brookfield Asset Management recently announced Brookfield Ventures, a VC arm that made its first investment of $15 million in BuildingConnected in 2018. Colliers International has partnered with Techstars to accelerate and invest in PropTech start-ups, and MetaProp is advising RXR Realty as it launches its own $50 million fund.

As we mentioned earlier, agile family businesses such as Rudin Management, Berman Enterprises, and Moinian Group have started their own PropTech venture funds, but established general VC funds have also been moving into PropTech. We see more of these almost every week now, not just in North America but also around the world. Moreover, early visionaries such as Trinity Ventures and RRE have been joined by familiar names such as Sequoia, Thrive Capital, and Andreesen Horowitz, which have directed significant capital to PropTech deals.

A Changed Environment

It took longer than might be expected, but the PropTech investment outlook has changed radically since Flint sought funding for Trulia, and even since Mandel hunted capital for CompStak. The number and size of PropTech deals began to rise in 2013, according to CB Insights, and investment has skyrocketed during the last three years.[83] In 2015, global venture-capital investments in PropTech companies totaled around $1.8 billion, according to RE:Tech.[84] In 2016, it more than doubled, to $4.2 billion, and in 2017, it tripled, shooting up to $12.6 billion.[85]

The lion's share of that investment has occurred in the US, according to Pitchbook, which tracks equity markets, including venture capital. The platform recorded $5.36 billion invested across more than one hundred PropTech deals in the US during 2017, a gargantuan increase over the $41 million invested in the seven deals it tracked in 2008.[86]

Accurate numbers are notoriously hard to come by in this fast-moving space, and we aren't vouching for any particular set, but the massive increase in investment dollars is clear.

If any serious investors were still oblivious to the trend by 2017, they got a wake-up call when SoftBank's "Vision Fund" put $3 billion into WeWork, with another $1.4 billion going to its subsidiaries. SoftBank Chief Masayoshi Son also pledged $867 million to Katerra—a company using technology to streamline construc-

---

83   "Real Estate Tech Funding Reaches New Highs In 2016," CB Insights, January 18, 2017, cbinsights.com/research/real-estate-tech-startup-funding.
84   Rey Mashayekhi, "VC Funding in Real Estate Tech Leaped to $12.6B in 2017: Report," Commercial Observer, January 3, 2018, commercialobserver.com/2018/01/vc-funding-in-real-estate-tech-leaped-to-12-6b-in-2017-report.
85   Ibid.
86   Dana Olsen, "The 14 most active VC investors in US real estate tech," Pitchbook, August 28, 2018, pitchbook.com/news/articles/the-top-14-vc-investors-in-real-estate-tech.

tion—$450 million to digital real estate brokerage Compass, and $120 million to Lemonade.

The investment climate has certainly changed, but why?

Investment is an integral part of the PropTech ecosystem, inseparable from partnerships and community. The reasons that investment in the space has taken off overlap with the reasons we presented for the rise of PropTech generally, in chapter 2, "Why PropTech Now?"

Investment is an integral part of the PropTech ecosystem, inseparable from partnerships and community.

As we noted in that chapter, investors have come to realize the potential of a massive industry that has lagged on technology. Real estate represents $38 trillion in the US alone, more than 13 percent of GDP.[87] A number of big wins from the likes of Zillow, Redfin, Trulia, and Airbnb have proven that PropTech can produce serious returns, just as technology investments in other realms have. FinTech in particular has been an important model and influence both because it developed an ecosystem that has made money for investors and because it is closely tied to real estate. Few experts understand FinTech better than Nadeem Shaikh, founder and former CEO of Anthemis Group, an investment company that has grown bullish on PropTech.

"I think the sophistication of the value chain becomes quite important," Shaikh told us in an interview. "Building an ecosystem of like-minded investors who see the world through a similar lens,

---

87   "Big Data: Disrupting Traditional Commercial Real Estate Management," AGC Partners, accessed January 2019.

or at least an adjacent lens, and can be complementary becomes very important because you want diversified capital there."

The fear of losing revenue also has spurred investment in PropTech as much as the lure of producing it. The rapid growth of competitive threats posed by companies such as Opendoor, WeWork, Airbnb, and Compass have gotten the attention of the real estate industry, which has begun investing money in PropTech start-ups partly for the potential return but mostly as a way to find solutions and up its tech game. For incumbents, investment in and partnerships with PropTech start-ups is essentially a way to boost R&D spending with less risk and better results.

Globalization, as we mentioned in chapter 2, has also played a pivotal role. The biggest US PropTech deal of 2017 came from SoftBank, a Japanese company, which as we were writing this, took a $45 billion infusion from Saudi Arabia for its second $100 billion Vision Fund, bringing the total Saudi investment in SoftBank to $90 billion. PropTech innovations have global implications, and capital for real estate technology is now flowing from all over the world—London, Germany, China, and India, as well as New York and California.

Finally, just as we have noted that innovation begets innovation, investment begets investment. As capital flows into PropTech start-ups, their valuations tend to increase. This trend is augmented by the rise of accelerators, mentors, advisors, partnerships, events, and other elements of the burgeoning PropTech ecosystem boosting the odds for entrepreneurs. Higher valuations mean that VCs can sell their equity at a profit, which encourages them to invest in more PropTech start-ups, and often, to up their stakes in portfolio companies. This leads to further investments, which increases their valuation, which … you get the idea.

Definitions and Dynamics

With thanks to Julia Arlt and PwC for their contribution.

In a moment, we'll talk a bit about our investment process at MetaProp, but first, we'd like to back up to present some basic definitions and dynamics. This will be review for many readers, but since we designed this book to be accessible to anyone interested in PropTech, we don't want to throw terms around without defining them. If this section is old-hat, we invite you to skip ahead to the next, but for readers new to the space, here are a few basic, commonly used terms.

Founder, entrepreneur

We have used these terms interchangeably, as most people in PropTech do. This is the seed that grows into the company, the person with the idea for a new product or service, or the chutzpah to turn someone else's idea into a scalable business. Some start-ups run with a single founder, but most develop with two or more.

Venture capital

The financing typically provided to start-ups, which, because they have no track record, would have trouble getting bank loans or other forms of financing. In return for an investment, start-ups give venture capitalists, or VCs, equity (an ownership stake) in their companies. Venture investments offer the potential for high returns but also carry high risk.

Limited partner (LP)

An investor in a VC fund. Above, we mentioned that CBRE and Cushman & Wakefield, among others, invested in our $40 million fund, MetaProp Ventures II. This makes them our limited partners (LPs).

Angel investor

An individual investor in a start-up. Angel investors might be friends and family members, or high-net-worth individuals with an interest in real estate and/or tech. Often, they were entrepreneurs themselves. They tend to get involved early on, in the "seed stage" (see "funding rounds" below). Before cofounding MetaProp, Zach had become the top angel investor in US PropTech.

Funding rounds

These labels help define where start-ups are in their journey and help categorize VC funds. The old system was simply to assign letters to each round of venture capital that start-ups raised. The first round was series A, the second, series B, and so on. At some point, investors began calling the first round the seed round, or series seed, and then, often, preseed. Additional investments by the same players, after they've funded a round, are now sometimes numbered. So, after series C might come series C-1.

VC stages

Venture capitalists most often define themselves by the stage in a start-up's life when they tend to invest. At MetaProp, we are early-stage experts, focused on the preseed through series A rounds, when companies are getting started, developing products, piloting, and testing markets. Midstage VCs are focused on start-ups in series B and later financing rounds. By this point, the companies, typically, have proven themselves, at least to some degree; they often have a viable product and are trying to scale. Late-stage VCs usually come into the picture when a company is successful but looking to raise money, perhaps on its way to an IPO or acquisition.

Exit

A liquidation event that allows investors to cash out. The most common exits include (1) those occurring as the result of an acquisition, in which another company purchases the start-up and the investors are paid off; and (2) those occurring as the result of an IPO, in which the start-up offers shares of stock for sale to the public.

Early-Stage Investment

Here, again, we will focus on the niche that is both the most difficult part of investing to navigate and our forte at MetaProp: early stage. With the invaluable help of our partner Zak Schwarzman, who leads our venture activities, we will give readers a rough overview of our process and share some of the secret sauce that has allowed MetaProp's investmentsto flourish. Our goal here is not to be self-serving. Instead, we hope that revealing some of our methods and insights will begin to open a window on PropTech investing for those new to the space.

First, a few stats: as we write this, MetaProp has so far invested in close to fifty start-ups through two VC-fund vehicles, MetaProp Ventures I and MetaProp Ventures II. As individuals, we have invested in another sixty or so start-ups, so the organization and its principles have invested in around one hundred start-ups total. So far, we've focused intensely on early-stage PropTech, which means start-ups in preseed, seed, and series-A funding rounds. Our typical initial investment ranges from $50,000 to $2 million. However, over the life of a company, we expect to invest a total of $3 million to $4 million in it.

Deals come to us through any number of channels, sometimes because of our reputation in the PropTech ecosystem, and sometimes because of relationships we've cultivated. Those relationships have developed through the network of more than ninety founders we back at this point: our coinvestors in real estate technology, our limited partners (a list that includes some of the top global real estate firms), and our other connections in real estate. Our advising activities often lead to potential deals. Additionally, of course, the MetaProp Accelerator at Columbia University gives us, as investors, the first look at an incredible pool of entrepreneurial talent that we are cultivating and mentoring.

Once a potential deal appears, we do a lot of what our partner Zak Schwarzman calls "quick scrubbing," an initial screen to qualify a start-up. Many of the ideas that we see are not quite ready for prime time. If we're going to pass on a deal, we try to make that assessment quickly. We don't want to waste anyone's time. However, we often do so with the hope that, down the line, a start-up will be back in a more viable state.

We look at three things for our initial screen: (1) people, (2) product, and (3) market.

PRODUCT

Outsiders are often surprised to learn that of our three prime criteria, the product is the least critical. The earlier the stage, the less important the product, and the early stage is where we live. Not that product is unimportant. Even in the pre-seed and seed stages, the product is the kernel that might grow into a success; it's the locus of potential.

We look more at figuring out an investment thesis, though, than at the particulars of a product in the early stage. What big change has occurred in the world that will enable these entrepreneurs to bring a new concept to life where others have failed? That might be a change in the state of technology. Consider, for instance, the many companies born during the last decade because we all began carrying around continuously connected, handheld computers. It might be a change in cloud computing, customer preferences, or the departmental landscape. Perhaps a group of partners now exists to enable things that couldn't be done previously.

In the absence of a big change enabling something new, we ask, what did everybody get wrong before these founders? Can they lay out a nuanced vision of the competitive landscape? Where have incumbents or other upstarts tried and failed, and why is this start-up's vector into the market different? The other possibility is that no one else has ever thought of the founders' idea, but that's rarely the case.

Here is MetaProp's PropTech taxonomy based on the real estate value chain described in chapter 4. It's worth revisiting because it's an important tool in our investment strategy. Our categories are:

1. analysis and financing

2. space ID and listing

3. site selection and negotiation

4. diligence

5. development and construction

6. process automation

7. space usage and management

8. payments and services

Early in our screening, we begin thinking about where a potential product or problem fits in our schema. Locating it in this way highlights where a start-up might add value and earn revenue within the industry, and it gets us thinking about market potential, which we'll get to in a moment.

PEOPLE

Perhaps the most valuable thing about product at this point is that it suggests how founders are approaching a problem or envisioning an opportunity. In early-stage PropTech, we are certain that the product will evolve, if not change entirely, over the course of a company's life, so we focus much more on people. We want founders who are obsessed, but with the problem, not the product.

According to Zak:

> When the market gives feedback to people who care first and foremost about the problem, they will adapt because they just want to solve the problem. They will persist to find the best solution. Entrepreneurs obsessed with how creative and special their solution is will try to ram it down the market's throat, regardless of feedback. So you want people who are fairly flexible.

We look for a team that has a vision they can articulate, some track record of success, and what is often called in our business a unique superpower, which is what makes the team uniquely positioned to bring their vision to life. This might be a set of experiences, a body of knowledge, a unique network, domain expertise, demonstrable influence, or something else that will get this project off the ground.

This investment process isn't like researching stocks; it's relationship based, long-term, and personal.

This investment process isn't like researching stocks; it's relationship based, long-term, and personal. We work with start-ups for years. We try to get a sense of who entrepreneurs are, how they operate, and how they deal with feedback and adversity. How adaptable, coachable, and persistent are they? Will they grow over time?

MARKET

Of the three elements we're assessing, *market* ranks a close second behind *people*. In the venture capital model, we aim for investments that will have outsized outcomes because we have to offset the risk inherent in early-stage start-ups. Another way to think of this is that we need our winners to be really big.

Having said that, because real estate is the biggest asset class and a massive, multifaceted industry—more than 13 percent of GDP, as we've noted—seemingly small solutions often have tremendous market potential.[88] Simple products and modest advances in technology also can turn into surprisingly big moneymakers because real estate tech has lagged for so long.

When he started CompStak, Michael Mandel took an existing system for trading comp information among commercial brokers and moved it online. Spacious Cofounder Preston Pesek noticed armies of mobile workers and endless empty restaurant space and built a platform to connect them. The founders of Radiator Labs addressed the perennial problem of wasteful, uncontrollable radiators with an affordable enclosure using familiar technology.

These and many PropTech products are, at their core, relatively simple. They offer elegant solutions to specific problems, but they have huge market potential. In New York alone, consider the number of radiators, the amount of office space being leased and sold, the number of restaurants empty before five o'clock in the evening, and you get the picture. Our rule of thumb is that the potential revenue

---

88   "Big Data: Disrupting Traditional Commercial Real Estate Management," AGC Partners, accessed January 2019.

or end market value has to be in the billion-dollar-plus range to make an investment worthwhile. In real estate, you don't have to be working on the next Zillow or Airbnb to hit that mark.

Here again, thinking about where a start-up falls in our taxonomy, based on the real estate value chain, points to market potential. Putting a solution in the right value-chain bucket helps us assess potential competition and bring the idea to our corporate partners for feedback. Classifying solutions in this way as part of our analysis can also lead to an expansion of market possibilities. It's not unusual, for instance, for us to see a team working with the office market in mind, categorize them as, say, process automation, and then point out that their solution has potential applications in retail and hospitality as well. Our taxonomy becomes a tool to maximize market potential.

PROCESS

After an initial screening that delves into the elements mentioned above, we have a conversation that rises to the partner level at MetaProp. If there is interest, we quickly go to our network of strategic limited partners and others in our real estate industry network. These are potential customers and partners for the company in question, so their opinions and feedback are invaluable. We also might put a limited partner or other industry executive in direct contact with the young company, which is great for everyone involved. The start-up team meets a prospective customer, the industry partner gets an advanced look at a product that could help its business, and we get feedback on a potential investment.

If the idea looks compelling and we can start to articulate an investment hypothesis, Zak sends it around to our partnership with three big items: (1) a list of the basic premises one must believe for the hypothesis to be true, (2) major areas for inquiry (the questions yet to be answered), and (3) the remaining steps his team wants to take (people to consult, areas to explore, etc.). The full partnership weighs in with feedback and questions and then Zak's deal team goes to work, doing further analysis, reference checks, and background work, talking to more experts, and so on. If the deal team has a strong conviction, they send the deal to the full partnership with a more robust investment recommendation. We make sure that every partner has spoken with the entrepreneur, and then we vote on the deal.

Early-stage companies move quickly, so smart investors must be nimble. The process we're describing typically takes about two weeks, but if necessary, we can turn an investment decision around within forty-eight hours. How is that possible?

According to Zak:

> You build up a filter and when you've done as much volume as we have, it becomes pattern matching and recognition on one level. Of course, over time, you build up a sense of people, a kind of sixth sense. But when we see a great entrepreneur eyeing a sizable market, that can be the biggest determining factor, and everything else is supporting.

Our investment process is inextricably linked with partnership and community. Remember our Venn diagram? So, the decision to invest is only the start of the journey. We leverage our relationships and vast network to provide entrepreneurs with mentors, coaching, and pilots with some of the top names in real estate. These benefits, which we explored in detail in the previous two chapters, are the real key to winning deals.

Zak breaks the quest for great investments into three categories: find the deal early, before anyone else can, and fund it; find it later and pay more for it; or convince entrepreneurs to take your capital at a lower price because you're providing added value. MetaProp is always in the first and last categories. We find the deals early, often quite early, and we provide added value for entrepreneurs, including a sandbox of fifteen billion square feet where ideas can be tested across a powerful base of limited partners. Those partners have demonstrated a commitment to technology and, on our recommendation, want to see and try it before it's fully baked.

When MetaProp gets into deals, we offer our coinvestment partners, which include some of the best firms in general venture capital, market-specific due diligence. We can tell them that there is demand, or likely will be, for this product, and this team is the best that we have found to back in this space.

After the first investment, we plan on making more follow-on investments to give a company the best possible odds of success. Typically, we start with $50,000 to $2 million, but as noted, over the long haul, we will invest a total of $3 million to $4 million in a company. This means that in our second fund, MetaProp Ventures II, a good portion of the capital may be reserved for follow-on investments.

We also follow up after the initial investment with distribution assistance, which in PropTech has been the drag for even successful companies. How do you sell into real estate, which has resisted technology historically, and even as PropTech heats up, remains a highly fragmented customer base with an opaque decision-making process?

We provide a shortcut, which, particularly in early-stage distribution, can be the difference between winner and also-ran.

As investors, we think like entrepreneurs, not surprisingly, given our backgrounds. Before the two of us started MetaProp, we started, grew, and exited companies. We worked extensively in real estate, in tech, and at their intersection. We have the judgment not only to help start-ups form partnerships and get investments but also the right deals at the right times. Sometimes this means helping a new company steer clear of a pilot or investment that could stifle growth or tie their hands at a critical stage. This is more art than science and comes from a unique set of skills and experiences that give us confidence in a relatively new and rapidly changing space that can be extremely difficult to navigate.

PropTech Investment in Early Innings

We have hardly scratched the surface of PropTech investment in this chapter. We could easily write another book just on this subject. As Constance Freedman, one of the top venture capitalists in the space, noted in an interview with us, the topic is full of complexity.

"I think that people need to understand [PropTech]," said Freedman, who after successfully launching and leading Second Century Ventures, the National Association of Realtors' strategic investment arm, started her own venture fund, Moderne Ventures, in 2015. "There's certainly hype about what it could be, but there are a lot of nuances that, for someone who is not in the industry, are not necessarily obvious."

As we have said repeatedly, knowledge is money as well as power, and when it comes to investing especially, there is no substitute for knowledge.

"I think that people should understand their investments," Freedman told us. "That's key, the true market size and market opportunities that exist given the constraints and regulatory issues … You have to understand the industry to make wise decisions."

Jeffrey Berman, a general partner in Camber Creek, one of the most respected VCs in the business, agrees. In an interview with us, he points out that the depth of knowledge and analysis needed to make smart PropTech investments is difficult to come by on a part-time basis, even for, say, an established real estate company:

> The problem with that type of investor is that unless they have a team dedicated full-time to evaluating opportunities in the CREtech space, they're analyzing deals in a vacuum. So, the best and, admittedly, somewhat self-serving advice I can give is that if you're interested in investing in PropTech, become an LP at one of the sector-specific funds in the space whose literal job it is to parse through all of the opportunities.

Renowned angel investor Joanne Wilson, CEO of Gotham Girl Ventures and creator of the eponymous blog, recommended when talking with us that PropTech investors think long-term, not aiming for a speedy exit, and develop a consistent strategy:

> I like to own 1 percent of the business. I don't like to put money into companies that are valued over $5 million dollars in the post. I'm a very early-stage investor. I will continue to follow on if the company is doing what I hope it's doing and the term sheets align, or are not egregious—if they make sense and I can still make money as the company moves forward on that particular route.

For investors with the ability to intelligently sort through what can seem like an avalanche of opportunities in real estate technology today, Berman, like many of the experts we interviewed for this book, believes that PropTech will continue to offer great returns. Our research supports his take: 96 percent of respondents to MetaProp's Mid-Year 2018 Global Confidence Index said they planned to make the same number of PropTech investments or more during the next year.

"I would posit that we're at the tip of iceberg, simply because tech hasn't saturated all aspects of the 'real estate experience,'" Berman told us. "The real estate industry is still, by and large, at version 1.0. From transactions to operations to management, it's business as usual more often than not."

Despite the rising tide of capital in PropTech, according to Ryan Freedman (chairman and CEO of Corigin Ventures) in an interview with us, real estate technology still has immense room for growth relative to other industries:

> Sure, we've seen funding pick up in the past few years, but it's been very concentrated in big names: Airbnb, WeWork, Compass. When you compare the *cumulative* funding of PropTech versus financial services or healthcare during the past ten years, it's not even close. We are in early innings here.

Many ask how MetaProp conducts diligence on potential startup investments. The process is a mix of science and art; we could write an entire book on the subject! The following pages include a few select examples of basic diligence and investment process tools that our firm has used over the years. Be sure to check proptech101.com for additional investment resources and pro tips. In the meantime, happy hunting!

PRE INVESTMENT CHECKLIST

Your Name: _____

Company Name: _____

Requirement	Initials
Pitch and any other relevant round- or company-related documents received and archived	
Market need/opportunity validated	
Competitive analysis and other initial research completed	
Financial model reviewed	
Technical roadmap reviewed	
Use of funds clarified	
Due diligence questionnaire completed	
Founder conversation with Lead Partner	
Founder conversation with Other Partners	
Full leadership team met	
Reference (personal + customer + vendor) calls conducted	
Outreach within MetaProp network (SMEs + off-list references/common connections)	
Investment documents reviewed by counsel	
Investment summary created	
Background check conducted (and/or verified that another investor has completed this step)	
Updates made in CRM system, including link to digital folder(s)	
Term sheet created	

GENERAL REFERENCE CALL TEMPLATE

Reference, MM/DD/YY

1. How long have you known person?

2. What was your relationship to person?

3. What are person's greatest strengths?

4. What motivates person (fear of failure, money, renown, personal goals)?

5. How does person motivate others (fear, example, rewards, strong vision)?

6. How does person deal with failure (blame others, overly-hard on self, spin control)?

7. How does person make decisions? What percentage of weight does person place on facts versus intuition versus relationships?

8. What could person improve (how would you complement his strengths with other management team members)?

9. Have you ever had any reason to question person's integrity, honesty, or follow-through on their word?

10. Would you feel comfortable investing in a company that person is leading?

11. Is there anything else you would like to say about person that I have not asked? If you were investing, what else would you want to know about person?

12. Is there anyone else we should talk to about person? Is there anyone with whom person does not get along?

13. How does this person work with the investors? What are their expectations and communication style?

QUICK DILIGENCE QUESTIONNAIRE

Market

- What problem/issue are you trying to solve? What is the need's urgency and intensity?

- Who is your target customer? What is the market size of this customer set (total $, total #, CAGR, etc.)?

- What relevant head- and/or tailwinds characterize the market you're pursuing right now?

- How do you see yourself and/or the market evolving over the next decade?

Competition

- Who are your direct competitors? Where are they in terms of company evolution/timeline?

- How do you intend to differentiate yourself against key competitors? What is your competitive advantage?

- What substitutes exist and how well do they solve the customer's current need?

Product

- What product development stage are you in? Please share details regarding the product roadmap with major feature and commercial milestones.

- How do you protect your IP? How difficult is it to build a similar product and compete in this space? What hurdles exist for new entrants?

Team

- Please list all current team members and their roles, as well as any past team members with equity.

- What skill gaps exist in your team? How do you hope to fill these?

Business Model/Unit Economics

- What is your monetization strategy?

- How are you pricing the product? What costs are associated with the product? What kind of margins do you intend on having short-term and long-term?

- What is your CAC (cost of acquisition) and LTV (lifetime value)?

- What does great market adoption look like for you? What will it take to get there once your product is in an ideal state?

Go To Market/Business Development

- What is your overall business development strategy?

- Do you have any live or pilot customers? What does your customer pipeline look like?

- What are your marketing and distribution channels?

- What kind of power do your vendors and/or strategic clients hold?

- What factors, processes, or stakeholders influence purchase decision?

References

- Please provide two references in each of the below categories:
    - Personal/professional
    - Investor
    - Customer

Financing

- Please share any past and current financing information (investors, valuations, round terms, etc)

- How do you intend to use current amount being raised?

Risks

- What legal or other risks exist in building and commercializing this product?

INVESTMENT SUMMARY

Deal Name: [Company name]

Investment Thesis

[Driving rationale behind the investment (e.g. opportunity to become the Zillow of Mexico/CompStak of India, highly technical team solving a niche but widespread and costly energy management problem, well-networked moonshot to create a commercial lending marketplace]

Company Overview

[Summary of the company, including the below]

- Vision:

- Product: [1-sentence description of initial product]

- Differentiation/advantage: [Why is this compelling?]

- Founders: [Why do you believe this team will succeed?]

- Raise: [Raising how much on what terms?]

Investment Opportunity

- Proposed investment: [$2,500,000]

- Round size: [$###,####]

- Terms: [Priced (incl. pre-money valuation, notable terms) or note (incl. cap, discount, dividend)]

- Composition: [Who else is in? Is anyone leading?]

- Pro Rata: [Have we reserved pro-rata rights via major investor threshold or via a side letter?]

Market Opportunity

[What specific market is the company addressing? Describe the dynamics of the market? Has there been any secular change in the market/technology that makes it particularly promising for this company to bring this solution to market now?]

Product

[Describe the company's product (and product vision if illustrative), particularly its key innovations/differentiating factors. What makes it special?]

Competition

[List major competitors (or categories of competitors w examples) and why this company has an advantage/superior approach]

Revenue Model

[If there is one. Or if one is probable/obvious]

Key Management

[Founding team members with relevant bios (i.e., demonstrate founder/product/market fit), superpower that will allow him/her to differentiate in market/have unfair advantage, priority hires]

Merits

[Bullet list the principle reason(s) that you believe this company has the potential to be a fifty-mulitple outcome]

Key Risks

[Bullet list the biggest risks that you see in this deal]

INNOVATION CONVERSATION

Ryan Freedman, chairman and CEO of Corigin

MetaProp: Can you give us a few facts about your business?

Ryan Freedman: Corigin is a multidisciplinary alternative investment firm with $500 million-plus in assets invested in real estate and venture capital. Our VC firm, Corigin Ventures, was founded in 2012, starting with a $20 million Fund I, and is currently deploying a $50 million Fund II. We were able to prove early that we could leverage our real estate asset base and real estate operating teams to add value to our early-stage PropTech investments.

Our typical deal is a $1 million seed investment. We have been intentional with our fund sizes to allow us the flexibility to both lead deals as well as collaborate with others. We learned, early on, the power of the lead and made sure our model could support high-conviction decisions by leading rounds and setting terms. We are also strategic in our follow-on strategy, reserving the majority of our capital to be deployed in series A and series B follow-on rounds of our most promising founders and companies. Today, we have over forty-five portfolio companies, of which roughly one-third are in property technology.

MetaProp: Do you focus on a particular niche, early-stage, late-stage, etc.?

Ryan Freedman: We are focused on leading and coleading seed-stage deals; we seek to be the most impactful partner at the earliest stages of a start-up's lifecycle. Both my partner David and I are entrepreneurs and have taken our own journeys to build businesses, mine in real assets and David's in consumer technology. We recognized how difficult the journey is but also recognized that regardless of product or industry, from seed to series A, start-ups are dealing with similar issues around talent, execution, and fundraising, and so, we have set out to build the venture firm that we wished we'd had supporting us through the early days of our start-ups. It is our product-market fit, and we have built our team and process around executing this strategy.

MetaProp: How and why did you get interested in investing in PropTech?

Ryan Freedman: I have been building microunits since before they were called microunits and innovating our real estate portfolio before the PropTech nomenclature existed. Our firm's culture has driven us to innovate and constantly improve upon our previous methods. We have been seeking to solve for pain points in our real estate portfolio and operation since the beginning, and the burgeoning PropTech ecosystem has allowed us to formalize our thesis and investments through our venture capital firm. It has been a powerful combination, to have the deep real estate expertise and network and be able to apply that to the companies we are investing in.

MetaProp: What is unique about investing in PropTech?

Ryan Freedman: The market size here is the big, obvious answer, but the ability to penetrate that market is guarded by old-school owners and operators. This has begun to shift dramatically in the last few years, and while there are leaders who are innovating, the ones who are not will quickly recognize that in order to compete they will have to bring their assets and operations up to the same level of service and efficiency. Because of the useful life of assets and their components, it will take decades for complete and mass adoption of everything to come. When you put that together with the market size, this is something that makes us think the opportunities here will exist for quite some time.

MetaProp: If you had to focus on one or two things, what would you say you look for most in a start-up?

Ryan Freedman: Because of our early-stage focus, we are investing in founders first, data and product second. We look for founder-market fit where these entrepreneurs possess a unique tie to the markets they are looking to disrupt or enable. After that, we make sure that their business possesses real unit economics. We are not interested in companies that only focus on growing their average users or their top line without sound economics behind their product.

MetaProp: What strategies do you use to assess a company with little or no track record?

Ryan Freedman: We are investing in people. We view EQ as one of our core competencies, and we look for the same from our founders. We believe that what differentiates the best entrepreneurs and investors is the ability and dedication to build meaningful, authentic relationships with all stakeholders.

MetaProp: What advice would you give to people considering investing in PropTech?

Ryan Freedman: Pick the right team, passionate entrepreneurs with founder-market fit, attacking a real pain point. For every deal or idea you see, there are multiple teams going after the same or similar problems, and if they aren't there today, there will be a new team going after it tomorrow.

CHAPTER EIGHT

The Future of Real Estate

"There is an incredible spectrum of opportunity. We are focused on global data and benchmarking, leading to increased liquidity, better governance, and improved decision making, which is quite exciting. Equally, we see incredible breakthroughs in building design, automation, usage that reflects modern trends and experience through IoT solutions ... The Internet of Things could have the biggest impact on real-time modeling for the consumption of real estate assets."

—Robert Courteau, CEO, Altus Group,
parent company of ARGUS Software

The rapid tech-enabled changes underway in real estate can be exciting and frightening. Thought leaders predict that, in the near term, more platforms will integrate, buildings will largely run themselves, autonomous vehicles will change the urban landscape, and most traditional real estate brokers will disappear.

———

We began this book by proclaiming that PropTech is remaking real estate. Due to the limitations of time and space, we have barely scratched the surface of the myriad changes occurring today, much less explored the ways in which technology might transform real estate tomorrow. We hope, however, that we have given readers a taste of how PropTech is increasing transparency and efficiency, focusing on the customer experience, saving money, and both creating and threatening revenue streams as it upends old models.

As Klaus Schwab, founder and executive chairman of the World Economic Forum, said in the passage we quoted in chapter 1, the fourth industrial revolution has no historical precedent and is moving "at an exponential rather than a linear pace."[89] Venture capitalist Albert Wenger of Union Square Ventures has a similar view. In an interview with us, he calls ours "a golden era of tech entrepreneurship," citing growth in the number of software engineers and academic programs serving the marketplace, as well as the proliferation of open-source software, tools, and languages, as factors.

The influx of capital and the rise of an ecosystem fostering start-ups are key elements in the development of PropTech, as we've explored, but it would not exist without an underlying revolution in technology. When we interviewed Robert Entin, executive vice president and CIO of Vornado Realty Trust, he expressed an envy common among technologists who are impressed by that revolution, partly because they studied at a time when the building blocks were much less wieldy. As Entin, who graduated from Penn in '77 and

---

89   Schwab, op. cit.

who returns each year to act as an alumni judge for senior projects, puts it:

> I'm so jealous because today a student can conceive of a senior engineering project and for the most part, given the cheapness of chip building and programmable ROM, and of course, cloud computing, and web servers, you can, basically, make what you want to make. In my day, you couldn't necessarily make it. When I was a junior or a sophomore, the professor walked in and said, "Class, this is an Intel 4004 chip, the four-bit processor. Here's the instruction set." It was, like, twenty bucks for the chip, and we were all blown away.

Entin knew that a powerful transformation would occur in real estate technology, as in other industries, though not exactly the form it would take. We feel the same way today. Artificial intelligence, which Entin writes about later in this chapter, is already transforming property management and other real estate functions, but we are at the very front end of AI property managers and agents using machine learning to accomplish what were, once, labor-intensive functions. What will the start-ups pioneering these AI solutions offer in five years, or even three?

Many experts think autonomous vehicles will be widespread within a decade. The proliferation of the automobile changed American culture and business in ways that are hard to overstate. This was particularly true of real estate, which was transformed with the rise of suburbia and the interstate highway system, both spurred by cars. What impact will the next automotive iteration have on the industry? Virtual reality and augmented reality have massive potential within real estate, where envisioning space is critical. Here, too, we have hardly begun to explore the possibilities.

Blockchain technology, which many know best from Bitcoin and other cryptocurrencies, is a sophisticated ledger that eliminates intermediaries, with a virtually unhackable system designed to prevent fraud and provide a complete history of all transactions. It has wide applications for titles, "smart contracts," public records, and other pieces of the real estate puzzle that remain cumbersome, inefficient, and expensive.

Zach predicted in 2017 that the first conveyance of title would shortly occur through blockchain, and it did, in South Burlington, Vermont. He also predicted that a building would be constructed entirely with autonomous machinery that year. This did not occur, though California hosted the first building project in which autonomous machines did the preconstruction excavation, grading, and padding.

No one knows exactly what's coming in real estate, though arming yourself with this book and delving into PropTech are good starts if you want to make educated guesses and bet intelligently. For this chapter, we asked a variety of experts to sound off on the technologies and innovations that they think will have the most influence on real estate in the future, or the ones that most intrigue them. It flows nicely from the previous chapter, in which the consensus among investors seems to be that PropTech investment is still in "early innings," said Ryan Freedman of Corigin when we spoke to him.

The progress that has been made during the last few years in automation, IoT technology, data analytics, artificial intelligence, virtual reality, robotics, 3-D printing, blockchain, and more is breathtaking. The pace of innovation in PropTech truly does seem to be moving at a pace that's exponential rather than linear, as Klaus Schwab put it.[90] Simply tracking the solutions is a full-time job, though, as Zach points out in the first piece below. One of the next big waves will likely be the emergence of a single platform that integrates and connects various other platforms and point solutions.

Readers should take comfort in the fact that whatever real estate solution they're dreaming of, the odds it exists or soon will are continually increasing.

Readers should take comfort in the fact that whatever real estate solution they're dreaming of, the odds it exists or soon will are continually increasing. PropTech is no panacea, but when you spend your weeks as we do, assessing an endless stream of start-ups that are boosting sustainability for buildings and cities, making workspaces more human, streamlining workflows, increasing transparency, and improving real assets in many other ways, it's hard not to be hopeful. No one knows just what the future holds in real estate, but we take heart from the predictions of our friends and colleagues in the rest of this chapter.

Robots Rising: AI, Voice, and Ambient Computing Will Boost Utility

ZACH AARONS, COFOUNDER, METAPROP

Several emerging trends including artificial intelligence, ambient computing, and voice recognition will advance the platforms that have proliferated in PropTech. Data integration and transparency

---

90 Schwab, op. cit.

also are developing in interesting ways, especially in commercial real estate technology, which is eager for a single dominant platform.

Until now, a bunch of different platforms have done different jobs for their customers, including lease administration, property management, work orders, basic accounting functionality, and valuation analysis. These functions have sat, for the most part, in siloed platforms, either cloud-based solutions or on-premises solutions. We're beginning to see a much greater level of integration between these platforms.

The goal of every large landlord is one platform to rule them all. I can't tell you which platform that's going to be, but I can tell you that customers want to log into one place, one dashboard, and have all their data, all their functions as real estate professionals, available there.

Google started out as a search engine but became much more: a platform where you have your e-mail, document storage and sharing, and in many cases, your telephone is integrated. Think of that evolution as the next model for whichever PropTech platform wins. I can't tell whether the one platform to rule them all will be a large digital incumbent, one of the legacy accounting players around for decades, or a PropTech upstart, which is the type of company that we're backing at MetaProp. Nonetheless, it's coming. Will the unifying platform come from Yardi, Realpage, and MRI, or from the VTSs of the world? All are jockeying for dominance.

The newer platforms are built on newer and more scalable technology stacks, so it is easier for them to process API [application program interface] integrations, but larger incumbents have more money and resources. They can just throw a bunch of engineers at the problem in a way that a more cash-strapped start-up can't. Either way, one or more companies, whether a property manager, systems incumbent, or newer, more data-driven cloud-based upstart, will create that single platform.

The other PropTech trend that you can expect much more of in the near term is ambient computing and voice recognition. Currently, all software work—work orders, ticketing, broker-landlord communication, tenant satisfaction, experience platforms—is done either on a desktop or in a mobile application. In the coming years, people will control these platforms by voice rather than fingertips.

Why does the rise of ambient computing and voice recognition matter? It's going to create an unprecedented level of efficiency in using PropTech software. It will continue to increase the efficiency of the professional and the customer. Voice recognition is going to become the major gesture through which customers interact with their software. Also, as voice recognition improves, as data quality improves, and as the algorithms analyzing that data improve, the robots will improve the quality of their work. Unlike human brains, artificially intelligent brains don't have physical neural processing limits for computation. Robots can learn exponentially. They're coming for us.

A new, much thicker layer of artificial intelligence will infiltrate almost every aspect of PropTech. It will replace a lot of the tasks currently performed by humans on the software platforms that replaced pen, paper, and fax. A work order, for example, used to be manually written up and submitted. It still is, only it's now written in a different (digital) way, put in a database, and stored forever. That data can be used in a number of accretive ways that it couldn't when the medium was pen and paper.

However, the rise of artificial intelligence will obviate the need for the customer to "hand" input a lot of the data, a current bottleneck. For a while, that artificial intelligence will be a friend to us, but ultimately, as we know from the *Terminator* movies, AI is no long-term friend to humans. It will begin displacing lower-level jobs in the real estate industry: data entry and such things as rent collection. I believe that in the future, those and other tasks will be replaced by artificial intelligence.

Combining ambient computing, artificial intelligence, and voice recognition will create a game-changing utilization for the software platform.

Most Traditional Real Estate Brokers Will Be Gone in Ten Years

PETE FLINT, FOUNDER, TRULIA;
MANAGING PARTNER, NFX

A technology tsunami is rolling over residential real estate. It's already washed over low-lying areas such as information, communication, and search. And it's moving to higher and higher ground: operations, brokerages, property maintenance, and construction. The role of the real estate agent will change, and most traditional brokers will be gone in ten years' time. As investors watching this space, we're focused on three key areas: the transaction, alt living, and bricks and bolts.

During the decade from 2005 to 2015, tech advances made massive amounts of information available to consumers. Still, transactions remain shockingly antiquated: it takes months and tens of thousands of dollars to buy or sell a home, and yet, in less than three minutes, with a few taps from my phone, I can get an Uber at my doorstep or book a hotel in Botswana. This next decade, from 2015 to 2025, will be about the transaction, with consumers turning to platforms that are faster, easier, and more affordable.

The empowerment that technology is bringing to the real estate transaction isn't just the result of consumer frustration, cost, and efficiency. Consumers are now in the driver's seat with access to much more information, which gives them confidence to try newer transaction services. Increasingly, the real estate brands that will be front-of-mind for consumers will be digitally native brands such as Zillow, Redfin, and Opendoor. Some traditional brands will transition to become digitally enabled platforms, but the rest will either team up with digital brands or drift into obscurity. For this reason, we are closely watching all efforts to streamline the transaction (including the iBuyer movement) and have already invested in Ribbon, which is working with traditional agents to facilitate cash transactions.

My prediction that most traditional real estate brokers will be gone in a decade is another way of saying that most real estate transactions will take place through alternative platforms. As this shift occurs, there will be much less fragmentation in the brokerage and company layer.

Another trend we're following is the rise of alt living, which represents a dramatic change in the demand side: people are marrying later, having children later, buying houses later, and renting longer. Yet the supply side of the market remains fairly static. On an analog level, this makes sense: houses are physical objects, and they're hard to change. But we're seeing a crop of tech-enabled start-ups that are transforming and repurposing physical spaces. These businesses are creating digitally enabled living solutions that cater to coliving arrangements, the rise of digital nomads, and so on. Consumers are crying out for these solutions, which are a tremendous departure from the traditional ways in which properties have been rented.

The third area we see tech flooding is bricks and bolts. Construction, maintenance, and property management make up an enormous segment of the economy. The annual sales for Home Depot and Lowe's alone is approximately $170 billion. The investment in this area is enormous, with over $1 trillion spent on construction in the US annually. As the tidal wave of tech continues to rise in real estate, and with further advances in robotics and computer vision, I believe that significant software-infused players will be successful here as well.

PropTech Enabling Faster Space, Flexible Terms, More Energy

LISA PICARD, PRESIDENT AND CEO, EQ OFFICE

A fundamental shift is occurring within commercial real estate. Our customers' business has changed and keeps changing, and as a result, the CRE product that they need must change too. Real estate owners have for the most part looked at the capital markets as their customers, which runs counter to the needs of the core customers leasing, or call it *borrowing*, our assets. Those customers want a different product, something far more fluid that actually helps them operate their businesses, address the changes they're facing, and be successful.

Technology will help commercial real estate change in three areas where the industry has largely failed up to now: providing space faster, providing more flexible leases, and providing a more experiential workplace. Technology also is altering customer acquisition channels. As it increases transparency and allows owners to get perfect information in real time, intermediaries become less important, and real estate companies will increasingly market directly to consumers.

The time frame in which customers need to decide about and procure space is much tighter than it used to be. They can't necessarily say, "Oh, I've got a lease coming up in a year. Let's start looking." If they look that early, they don't really know how much space they need. When they know how much they need, they need it much faster than they used to. They also don't know how long they're going to need space for. Business cycles used to be longer. You could do a five-year or seven-year plan. Today, a business can barely do a six-month plan before it completely changes, so why would it sign a ten-year lease? Many are still pushed into ten-year leases, "bought off" with a tenant improvement allowance, more money, free rent, various perks to force them into an asset they don't want. When you step back, the system actually costs everyone money.

It's also really critical for organizations to create workplaces that have energy, environments that provide an experience, because workspace is now all about attracting and retaining the talent. WeWork has struck a chord because they're hitting on all three of these things. JP Morgan can go to WeWork and say, "Hey, we're a bank. We don't know how to create spaces that attract young people." Amazon or Facebook can get space in a month instead of six or eight. A start-up can sign for three months or three years.

The challenge for WeWork will be staying power. They'll have to continue to innovate their product. In the industry overall, PropTech will facilitate the productization of real estate. Instead of one product with one term length, we will parse that out and offer the market different products with various terms. Some users will want a ten-year lease, and they'll have the most ability to customize. By the time you get down to users who want to commit to six months or a year, the product will be more like classic office space, or an apartment, where we say, "Here they are, which one do you want?" Using technology to understand customer preferences will be critical because if we get the ready-made space wrong, just as apartment owners do, we will have trouble re-leasing it.

The tech-enabled focus on customers is also moving us from a B2B model to more of a B2C model. The need for brokers arose because of a lack of trust and transparency, but as technology allows for good information about transactions in real time, we will make more direct connections to customers and build more customer awareness of the product ourselves. Instead of the CEO of a real estate company marketing through the identity of another company, we will, increasingly, market directly to customers whose HR departments are driving decisions because they're focused on what inspires the talent.

The Rise of AI and the Self-Running Building

ROBERT ENTIN, EXECUTIVE VICE PRESIDENT, CIO, VORNADO REALTY TRUST

While I am a firm believer that blockchain will profoundly affect real estate one day, the next wave of technology that I think is really going to impact real estate will be artificial intelligence (AI). We already see it slowly creeping into almost everything we do, and into some of the software products that service the real estate industry. AI is seeping into organizations a little at a time, and one of its biggest impacts is in gradually creating buildings that will run themselves.

People have been harvesting building data for a long time. In the first wave, they harvested data but could not do much with it, other than deduce that they probably had a broken chiller or thermostat, and would have to figure it out for themselves. In the second wave, systems had alerts that told managers when something passed a designated point. In the third wave, machine learning can plug the system in, have it learn the building over time, spot variances and patterns, and tune itself, as well as tell you when something is wrong.

The paradigm shift in AI is that we're not programming algorithms with rules anymore. We're teaching the computer the rules of the game, whatever that game is, and then the letting it cycle through millions of iterations of the game, where it can determine the winners and losers, so to speak. And then it simply understands. It puts the winning cases in one bucket and the losing cases in another bucket, and says, "Okay, I want things that look like the winning cases." It's an enormous exercise in big data and pattern recognition and very different from the way we have always programmed computers.

For AI to be effective, you need massive amounts of data—millions and millions of iterations—and in real estate, there are lots of places where you don't have that. There aren't that many commercial leasing transactions in a given market, for example. The residential sales market, on the other hand, is ideal. Zillow and others have massive amounts of complicated data there: ZIP codes, demographics, income, pricing, zoning, trends. It's perfect for a machine-learning algorithm. AI also requires an ecosystem with rules that you can teach the computer.

One of the places with this sort of ecosystem and lots of data is a building. Thanks to IoT and mobile technology, energy management platforms that employ machine learning are springing up everywhere. They are really at the beginning stages now and can figure out on their own when something is wrong, alter set points, and/or take other actions.

How far are we from a building that largely runs itself? I believe that once innovation takes root, it multiplies rapidly, a version of Moore's law. Hopefully, in five years, building management systems (BMS) will look very different. One impediment is that the underlying software systems manufactured by large BMS vendors are often outdated, and building owners aren't yet at the table demanding better ones. The new platforms that clamp onto these systems are hamstrung by what's underneath.

Interestingly, Google, with its tens of millions of square feet, is very interested in this space. As with everything else, Google will go to the manufacturers and ask for BMS improvements, and if getting them is too hard or slow, the company will build its own system. I think it will be one of the forces that shakes up that industry. It wouldn't be surprising to see them in this business one day.

Tech Will Create Better Tenant Experiences, Space Utilization

JEFF BERMAN, GENERAL PARTNER, CAMBER CREEK

The real estate industry is such a greenfield opportunity for tech and there are so many things to be excited about that it's hard to focus on one. In general, however, I am a fan of technologies that create opportunities for positive behavioral changes, such as autonomous vehicles and urban mobility solutions. I've lived in New York for many years and I am still amazed by the sheer volume of pedestrian/vehicular/mass transit traffic that we have to contend with in the city. Autonomous vehicles, at every scale, have the potential to fundamentally change the way we interact with and plan our cities.

At the asset level, I am enjoying evaluating companies that are concentrating on the enrichment of the tenant/resident/end-user experience and the maximization of underutilized space. The latter is being driven by a shift in the way people are procuring and utilizing the spaces they inhabit: where they work, live, shop, are entertained, and so on. In the world of commercial real estate, coworking is a driving force behind the rethinking of how companies and people approach their real estate needs.

From a tenant's perspective, it is no longer necessary to commit to long-term contracts, even for larger companies. From the landlords' perspective, the opportunity to differentiate their properties from the competition's is coming from some of the more enterprising coworking companies. Those innovators are saying, "Let us manage X number of floors of your office building. We'll break the floors into a layout conducive to the ways in which people are actually working now, and we'll take a percentage of gross."

In that instance, the coworking company is essentially adopting the asset model of a light-hotel operator. In the multifamily sector, we're seeing a number of companies literally turning apartment buildings into hotels. One of our portfolio companies, WhyHotel, is taking a novel, tech-forward approach to a problem that almost every developer of a multifamily rental property has faced. WhyHotel operates pop-up hotels in new developments that are in the lease-up process, generating revenue in place of vacancy loss, all the while providing a tier-1, hotel-caliber experience in an apartment setting.

With WhyHotel on site, new tenants do not have to live for months in a largely vacant building, and owners like the fact that they're gaining a new revenue stream at a critical time. It's one of many examples of technology enabling both a better tenant experience and the monetization of underutilized assets, both pillars of PropTech and tomorrow's real estate industry.

Professionals' Predictions

"PropTech, in my opinion, has gained top-of-mind traction among real estate leaders. In Asia, the industry leaders I speak to recognize the impact of and potential opportunities for PropTech, thus driving a virtuous cycle of innovation to adoption to investment. In the longer term, this cycle is only going to grow faster. In the short term, many real estate leaders will have to get over the need to own PropTech platforms on an exclusive basis and embrace the idea of greater collaborations among many stakeholders."

Lim Ming Yan

former president and group CEO, CapitaLand

"We are excited about how multifamily and hospitality assets and operators continue to flirt with each other's traditional boundaries. Technology has started to close this gap and change these experiences, which is uprooting the fundamental rules of both asset classes. We are also excited about the ways that technology is changing how we access these assets. We are also cautiously optimistic about the future of real estate tokenization and have been quietly participating in the very early tokenizations in order to learn from the inside as this market begins to form."

Ryan Freedman

chairman and CEO, Corigin Ventures

"I'm seeing more start-ups than ever before, I think, for a few reasons: the cost of capital is at an all-time low for start-ups, computing innovations over the last two decades have made it easier than ever to start something, and New York's start-up ecosystem is the strongest it has ever been. The size of funding rounds also has increased. VCs invested over $5 billion in PropTech in 2017. It is too early to tell if these start-ups are failing at a greater rate. Large growth rounds have been raised in the last year, and PropTech companies appear to be scaling well, but a macro market event could change that. Venture is a cyclical business, and we have been on one side of the cycle for a long time."

Stuart Ellman

cofounder and general partner, RRE Ventures

"I think that PropTech will have a massive impact in the coming years. Probably we've learned from the financial industry. Five years ago, they did not work together with FinTech start-ups. The turning point came in 2017 when Amazon entered the finance industry. Today Amazon, Google, Microsoft, and IKEA invest in new solutions for real estate. They might also wake up the Dutch real estate industry."

Wouter Truffino

CEO and founder, Holland ConTech & PropTech

"We are going to have more and more bridges built in real estate, different pricing models, and different distribution models. There will be more and more mortgage lenders with different ways to underwrite and originate loans, and different financial products will be on offer, new ways to provide easier access to home ownership, and everything is going to have to keep up with that. Real estate is an ecosystem involving many different players, and if you can't keep up, then people aren't going to do business with you."

Patrick Burns

CEO, Spruce

"I am really excited about PropTech, which, as far as I can tell, is an industry ripe for growth and scale, exactly where we were in financial services eight or ten years ago. But PropTech's applicability is more global, much more geared toward mass play than FinTech. I think there's an opportunity to really think of this in a global landscape. You tee up your capital, your distribution, your relationship LPs, and so on, and you can have authentic technology that can have much more global play than was possible at the get-go in financial services."

Nadeem Shaikh

founder and former CEO, Anthemis Group

INNOVATION CONVERSATION
Brad Inman, chairman of the board, Inman

MetaProp: You and Inman have been pioneers in real estate tech media. Why did you decide to focus on real estate, and, increasingly, PropTech, in your coverage?

Brad Inman: I was a consumer journalist for many years for California newspapers and when the commercial internet came on the scene, I found an audience with the real estate industry, which I turned into Inman Today. The focus from the beginning, in 1996, was on how technology could reshape the industry to create a better consumer experience.

MetaProp: As a real estate media mogul, how do you view the importance and development of PropTech?

Brad Inman: *Mogul* is not a term I aspire to. However, it is clear to me that new technologies can take the grind out of the consumer real estate experience and make the transaction simpler, less expensive, and more transparent. It is that simple.

MetaProp: In your experience, during the last few years, how has the attitude of real estate executives changed in regard to PropTech?

Brad Inman: They once fought it, and sometimes illegally, bringing on the wrath of the US Justice Department. Now they must embrace it or die. They gave up so much to new tech companies because the industry was gripped by fear and arrogance. That attitude has disappeared as they have come to see the writing on the wall about the importance of new innovations to the industry.

MetaProp: How do you view the huge leap in venture-capital funding of PropTech over the last two years, from $4.2 billion in 2015 to $12.6 billion in 2017?

Brad Inman: It was inevitable, a huge category, ripe for change with lethargic incumbents.

MetaProp: What is the most challenging thing(s) about understanding PropTech start-ups and conveying that to your readers?

Brad Inman: Most start-ups enter the business with a grasp of the problem but are very innocent about how complex the solutions are. People do not move that often, so their infrequent real estate activity makes it tricky to offer a quick and easy tech path. The incumbents have a grip on the structure of real estate relationships and the data. Plus, they provide a valuable service, which consumers recognize. Most start-ups are successful when they partner with the industry. However, some more disruptive models have entered the picture, such as iBuyers, and they are taking a different path.

MetaProp: Which PropTech start-ups have most impressed you and why?

Brad Inman: The portals, the SaaS software solutions, predictive analytics, payment, and iBuyers.

MetaProp: Which traditional real estate companies are making the best use of PropTech start-ups?

Brad Inman: The postrecession indie brokers who embrace technology and operate with a different ethos about the consumer and the transaction. They are wired for change.

MetaProp: What do you see as the future of PropTech over the next couple of years?

Brad Inman: Mistakes, stumbles, progress, and then a complete overhaul of how real estate is transacted.

Embrace Tomorrow's Real Estate Industry

The most tech-savvy among us can be intimidated these days by the breadth and scope of PropTech. At MetaProp, we eat, breathe, and sleep real estate technology. It's our passion. Even so, tracking the trends, new start-ups, players, and key investments in early-stage PropTech takes immense effort from our highly specialized team. How are busy real estate practitioners with high-powered, full-time jobs supposed to make sense of this rapidly changing space?

We hope that this book is a good start, and that if you are new to the space it has identified some important dynamics and basic strategies that can help professionals move deeper into PropTech. There also exists a well-developed and constantly growing support structure that makes tracking trends and solutions, as well as making connections, easier.

The resources section following this conclusion highlights some of the tools that can help real estate practitioners navigate these complicated waters. Given the limitations of space and the lightning pace of change, we name only a handful of organizations or individuals in each category here: events, accelerators, VCs, influencers, and media outlets, among others. However, readers can follow the online address printed in our resources section for a more expansive and up-to-date list, checklists, and other collateral materials. They also can browse dozens more of MetaProp's Innovation Conversations online. (We published only a smattering of our ongoing dialogues with thought leaders in PropTech here.)

Don't think that you need to get your head fully around this space immediately or track every promising new start-up that might affect your sector. That will only make you crazy. We recommend that you simply get your feet wet. Start tracking some of the news sources and bloggers on real estate tech that resonate with you. Attend some PropTech events and begin networking.

Invite and enlist your colleagues and employees to engage with PropTech, too. We hope we have made the point that every company must now be a technology company, and that means that technology is now a part of everyone's job. The days of leaving tech matters to "the IT guy" are gone, thank goodness. PropTech can no longer be sequestered within one position or department. Whatever branch of real estate you work in, PropTech will affect your entire organization, creating myriad threats and opportunities. Companies that respond with a holistic digital strategy will have a growing competitive advantage.

The cliché that change is the only constant applies perfectly to PropTech. Solutions rise and fall as technology evolves. Assessing, enlisting, and changing it is a never-ending process, but tech is simply a tool, a way to effect strategy. The real point of PropTech is to embrace innovation, to make it a part of every synapse and sinew within the organization as it faces a future rife with opportunity, rather than retreating into a past replete with fear.

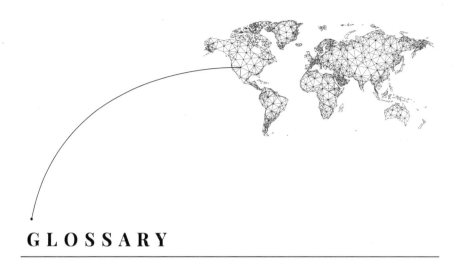

GLOSSARY

Accelerator is a fixed-term, cohort-based program that includes seed investment, connections, mentorship, educational components, and culminates in a public pitch event or demo day to accelerate growth.

Ambient computing is an ecosystem of internet-connected "things" that can intelligently respond in real time to business needs.

Application program interface (API) is a set of subroutine definitions, communication protocols, and tools for building software. In general terms, it is a set of clearly defined methods of communication among various components.

Artificial intelligence (AI) is the development of computer systems able to perform tasks that normally require human intelligence.

Augmented reality (AR) is a technology that superimposes a computer-generated image on a user's view of the real world, thus providing a composite view.

Automation is the use of largely automatic equipment in a system of manufacturing or other production process.

Big data is extremely large data sets that may be analyzed computationally to reveal patterns, trends, and associations, especially relating to human behavior and interactions.

Bitcoin is a type of digital currency in which encryption techniques are used to regulate the generation of units of currency and verify the transfer of funds, operating independently from a central bank.

Blockchain is a digital ledger in which transactions made in a cryptocurrency are recorded chronologically and publicly.

Bot, short for robot, is an automated program that runs over the internet.

Building management systems (BMS) is a computer-based control system installed in buildings that controls and monitors the building's mechanical and electrical equipment such as ventilation, lighting, power systems, fire systems, and security systems.

Client relationship management (CRM) is a technology for managing all of a company's relationships and interactions with customers and potential customers.

Cloud computing is the practice of using a network of remote servers hosted on the internet to store, manage, and process data, rather than using a local server or a personal computer.

Comparative marketing analysis (CMA) is an examination of the prices at which similar properties in the same area recently sold.

Coworking is the use of an office or other working environment by people who are self-employed or working for different employers, usually to share equipment, ideas, and knowledge.

Cryptocurrency is a digital or virtual currency designed to work as a medium of exchange.

Data analytics is a process of inspecting, cleansing, transforming, and modeling data with the goal of discovering useful information, informing conclusions, and supporting decision making.

Drones are unmanned aircraft guided by remote control or onboard computers.

Enterprise data platform (EDP) is the ability of an organization to precisely define, easily integrate, and effectively retrieve data for both internal applications and external communication.

FinTech describes new tech that seeks to improve and automate the delivery and use of financial services. At its core, FinTech is utilized to help companies, business owners and consumers better manage their financial operations, processes, and lives by utilizing specialized software and algorithms on computers and, increasingly, smartphones.

Heating, ventilation, and air conditioning (HVAC) is the technology of indoor and vehicular environmental comfort.

Global distribution system (GDS) is a computerized network system owned or operated by a company that enables transactions between travel industry service providers—mainly airlines—hotels, car rental companies, and travel agencies.

iBuyer is a company that will make you an offer on your home, sight unseen, based on a proprietary valuation model.

Internet of Things (IoT) is the interconnection via the internet of computing devices embedded in everyday objects, enabling them to send and receive data.

Machine learning is a field of artificial intelligence that uses statistical techniques to give computer systems the ability to "learn" (e.g., progressively improve performance on a specific task) from data, without being explicitly programmed.

Minimum viable product (MVP) is a product with just enough features to satisfy early customers, and to provide feedback for future product development.

Multiple listing service (MLS) is service used by a group of real estate brokers that allows each of them to see one another's listings of properties for sale.

Proof of concept is evidence, typically derived from an experiment or pilot project, which demonstrates that a design concept, business proposal, and so on, is feasible.

Read-only memory (ROM) is a type of nonvolatile memory used in computers and other electronic devices.

Real estate investment trust (REIT) is a company that owns, operates, or finances income-producing real estate.

Sharing economy is an economic system in which assets or services are shared between private individuals, either free or for a fee, typically by means of the internet.

Software as a service (SaaS) is a distribution model in which a third-party provider hosts applications and makes them available to customers over the internet.

Virtual reality (VR) is a computer-generated simulation of a three-dimensional image or environment that can be interacted with in a seemingly real or physical way by a person using special electronic equipment, such as a helmet with a screen inside or gloves fitted with sensors.

3-D Printing is the process of making three-dimensional solid objects from a digital file.

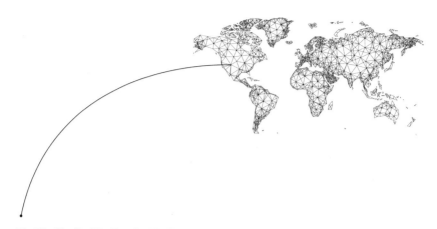

RESOURCES DIRECTORY

We partnered with Julia Arlt at PwC to develop a simple Resources Directory that can serve as a foundation for our readers' further PropTech investigations. This partial list is simply a starting point and, of course, will be quickly outdated. However, we intend to regularly refresh and update the Resources Directory. Please see the latest Resources Directory and other tools at our book website, proptech101.com.

CATEGORY	ORGANIZATION	BASE
Media	CRETech	North America
Media	Propmodo	North America
Media	PlaceTech	Europe
Media	RE:Tech	North America
Media	Founders Grove Capital	North America
Media	EG	Europe
Media	Infabode	Europe
Media	The Property Voice	Europe
Media	Konii - Digital Real Estate	Europe
Media	Nkf Media GmbH	Europe
Media	Poland Today	Europe
Media	PropertyNL	Europe
Media	TechNest.io - The Real Estate and Tech Show	North America

CATEGORY	ORGANIZATION	BASE
Media	PropTech News	Europe
Media	Silicon Luxembourg	Europe
Thought Leaders	Duke Long Agency	North America
Thought Leaders	Geek Estate	North America
Thought Leaders	James Dearsley	Europe
Thought Leaders	Antony Slumbers	Europe
Thought Leaders	Dror Poleg	North America
Thought Leaders	Mike DelPrete	North America
Thought Leaders	Dan Hughes	Europe
Associations and Hubs	CoreNet Global	Global
Associations and Hubs	REALPAC	North America
Associations and Hubs	REBNY	North America
Associations and Hubs	RICS	Global
Associations and Hubs	ULI Greenprint	Global
Associations and Hubs	UKPA	Europe
Associations and Hubs	Asia PropTech	Asia
Associations and Hubs	Spanish PropTech	Europe
Associations and Hubs	Holland ConTech and PropTech	Europe
Associations and Hubs	PropTechNL	Europe
Associations and Hubs	NAR	North America
Associations and Hubs	Real Estech	Europe
Associations and Hubs	PropTech SEE	Europe
Associations and Hubs	Czech and Slovak PropTech	Europe
Associations and Hubs	German PropTech Initiative	Europe
Associations and Hubs	PropTech Norway	Europe
Associations and Hubs	Nordic PropTech	Europe
Associations and Hubs	KTH Live-in lab	Europe
Associations and Hubs	PropTech Ireland	Europe
Associations and Hubs	SA PropTech	Africa
Associations and Hubs	Swiss PropTech	Europe
Associations and Hubs	Austrian PropTech Initiative	Europe
Associations and Hubs	PropTech Poland	Europe
Associations and Hubs	PropTech Canada	North America
Associations and Hubs	PropTech Russia	Europe
Associations and Hubs	PropTech Lab	Europe

CATEGORY	ORGANIZATION	BASE
Associations and Hubs	PropTech Baltic	Europe
Associations and Hubs	PropTech Finland	Europe
Associations and Hubs	ReTechDach	Europe
Associations and Hubs	Immowell Lab	Europe
Associations and Hubs	PropTech House	Europe
Associations and Hubs	EurAsia PropTech Initiative	Europe
Associations and Hubs	PropTech Japan	Asia
Associations and Hubs	IBREA	North America
Associations and Hubs	FIBREE - Foundation of Blockchain and Real Estate Expertise	Europe
Venture Capitalists	Borealis Ventures	North America
Venture Capitalists	Brick & Mortar	North America
Venture Capitalists	Camber Creek	North America
Venture Capitalists	Concrete Ventures	Europe
Venture Capitalists	Corigin Ventures	North America
Venture Capitalists	Fifth Wall	North America
Venture Capitalists	LeFrak Ventures	North America
Venture Capitalists	JLL Spark	North America
Venture Capitalists	MetaProp	North America
Venture Capitalists	Moderne Ventures	North America
Venture Capitalists	Navitas Capital	North America
Venture Capitalists	NineFour Ventures	North America
Venture Capitalists	PLD	North America
Venture Capitalists	RETV	North America
Venture Capitalists	Rudin Ventures	North America
Venture Capitalists	RXR Ventures	North America
Venture Capitalists	Simon Ventures	North America
Venture Capitalists	Taronga Ventures	Asia
Venture Capitalists	PropTech1 GmbH & Co. KG	Europe
Venture Capitalists	Loric Ventures	Europe
Venture Capitalists	Pi Labs	Europe
Venture Capitalists	BitStone Capital Management GmbH	Europe
Research	CrunchBase	Global
Research	CB Insights	Global
Research	PitchBook	Global
Research	Unissu	Global

CATEGORY	ORGANIZATION	BASE
Research	PWC	Global
Research	KPMG	Global
Research	Global PropTech Confidence Index	Global
Research	CRETech	North America
Research	RE:Tech	North America
Events	Asia PropTech Innovathon	Asia
Events	Builtworld Summit	North America
Events	CRETech	North America
Events	DisruptCRE	North America
Events	Future:PropTech	Europe
Events	Real Estate Innovation Network	Europe
Events	MIPIM PropTech NYC, Europe, Asia	Global
Events	PropTech Summit	Norway - Europe
Events	NYC Real Estate Tech Week	North America
Events	PropTeq	Europe
Events	Digital Disruption	Australia
Events	INMOTECNIA RENT	Europe
Events	blockchain-REAL	Europe
Events	PropTech Middle East	Asia
Events	PropTech360	Israel
Events	SIMA (Madrid International Real Estate Exhibition)	Spain - Europe
Accelerators/Incubators	ADAPT Accelerator	Asia
Accelerators/Incubators	Brigade REAP	North America
Accelerators/Incubators	Charter Hall Accelerator	Asia
Accelerators/Incubators	Colliers PropTech Accelerator powered by TechStars	North America
Accelerators/Incubators	MetaProp Accelerator at Columbia University	North America
Accelerators/Incubators	PiLabs	Europe
Accelerators/Incubators	Propell Asia	Asia
Accelerators/Incubators	Impulse Partners	Europe
Accelerators/Incubators	R-Labs Canada Inc.	North America
Accelerators/Incubators	Cushman & Wakefield and Plug and Play	Global
Accelerators/Incubators	PropTech Accelerator Israel	Asia